L O S T   I N   S P A C E

THE MAKING OF

LOST IN SPACE

PAT CADIGAN

TITAN BOOKS

THE MAKING OF LOST IN SPACE
ISBN 1 85286 906 2

Published by
Titan Books
42-44 Dolben Street
London SE1 0UP

First edition June 1998
10 9 8 7 6 5 4 3 2 1

British edition published by arrangement with HarperPrism, a division of
HarperCollins Publishers.

Book design and production: Jeanette Jacobs

Photo credits: Jack English and Milly Donaghy

British Library Cataloguing-in-Publication Data. A catalogue record for this book
is available from the British Library.

Titan's other film and TV related titles are available in all good bookshops, or
from Titan Books Mail Order, PO Box 54, Desborough, Northants, NN14 2UH.
You can also telephone 01536 763 631 with your credit card details. Please
quote MO/LS.

Printed and bound in Great Britain by Stephens and George Ltd, Merthyr
Industrial Estate, Dowlais, Merthyr Tydfil.

FOR THE ORIGINAL CHRIS FOWLER,

MY ONE TRUE LOVE IN ALL THE UNIVERSE

Acknowledgments and Thank Yous

The author owes an enormous debt of gratitude to: Cheryl Bickerton, Sam Black, and everyone on the visual effects team for aiding and abetting me with grace and good humor, finding time for me even when they were busy themselves; to Steven Begg, Nigel Stone, Mark Gardiner, and the rest of the model unit team for allowing me to spend several days in future Houston with them and giving me a peek through the camera; to Lacey Chabert, and Freda and Jack Johnson, who cheerfully made time for interviews when they could have been resting, shopping, or surfing the Web; to Norman Garwood and Vin Burnham for indulging me at great length with their knowledge and experience; to William Todd Jones for a wealth of insights, cinematic, theatric, and Welsh; to Tatiana Bicat for providing much needed visual reference material, even though it meant more work for her; to Verner Gresty for the fast and thorough education in puppets, muppets, and Blawps; to Anna Pinnock and her remarkable eyes for patiently explaining set decoration and construction; to Patric Scott for providing information and resources vital to the completion of this project, not to mention that chocolate dessert; to Akiva Goldsman for the warm welcome and for trusting me with a copy of the script; and finally to Angus Bickerton, Stephen Hopkins, and Gary Oldman, who most graciously and generously allowed me to observe the filming of a difficult special effects sequence. I hope to meet all of you again.

Thanks to everyone involved in the original *Lost in Space,* for making it so classic and unforgettable.

Also a tip of the hat to John Douglas for being a helpful and patient editor, and for not panicking, to my agent Merrilee Heifetz for thinking of me, and to Ellen Datlow and Jack Womack, for last minute accommodations and hospitality.

And an extra big thank-you to my own family—my son Bob, his Grandma Helen, and my husband Chris. Without them, I'd be lost.

The Robinsons of a 1997 foreseen from the mid-1960s.

On October 16, 1997, a family of five plus a young pilot in the United States Space Corps are launched into space from Houston, Texas. Recent interstellar probes have confirmed that the nearest star, Alpha Centauri, is orbited by two planets, Delta and Gamma, both of which can sustain human life. The family's mission—with the help of their pilot—is to establish a colony on one of the planets, as the first step in humanity's exploration of the universe. In theory, it was a wonderful idea, and it might even have worked, except that there was a seventh passenger on the spacecraft, a saboteur in the pay of a hostile government. His attempt to destroy the mission resulted in the spacecraft being thrown so completely off-course that it became hopelessly lost . . . in space.

The family and the pilot, all of them brilliant—well, smart enough, at least—healthy, well-adjusted, and cooperative, pulled together in their new mission to try to find a way back to Earth. In the meantime, they did their best to live as normal a life as possible, considering dangerous environments, visits from aliens—some friendly, some misguided, and some downright evil—and all manner of trouble from the saboteur, who is seldom brave, and is more conniving than brilliant. Fortunately, they have some cutting-edge technology to help them out: a robot, which can not only sense aliens about, but also talks . . . and learns.

That was the way the future was on September 15, 1965, a year teetering on the cusp of times that would, as the man said, be a-changin', but much more quickly and more furiously than most people were used to. JFK had been assassinated. Resistance to the war in Vietnam was growing, and the Civil Rights Movement was gathering momentum. Still to come were the assassinations of Robert F. Kennedy and Martin Luther King, Jr., the Democratic National Convention in Chicago, and the four dead antiwar demonstrators at Kent State in Ohio.

From that perspective, October 16, 1997, seemed almost impossibly far in the future, a distant time when, surely, we would vacation on Mars as routinely as we went to the beach or to the mountains. Never mind that we hadn't even landed a manned spacecraft on the moon yet. We were sure that by 1997 we would have advanced so far as to solve the problems of interstellar travel. And not just the scientific *how*, but the sociological *who* as well. Because in 1997, although a great deal would have changed, there would be one thing that had not, something so constant that no one would even think of questioning it: namely, the nuclear family.

October 16, 1997, has come and gone now and, as far as anyone knows, there has been no launch of a manned interstellar spacecraft from Houston, at least not in this particular branch of the multiverse. So, let's consider a slightly different scenario, from the perspective of post-October 16, 1997:

Sometime in the future, say a century or two from 1998, the end is much nearer than most people realize. The environment is now so damaged that it's impossible to live in the open. Protected from the deteriorating atmosphere by domes, and protected from the truth by propaganda, most people don't know that the Earth is literally finished—within two decades the planet will be completely out of air, water, and food. The only hope for the human race is emigration, a new start on another world.

Fortunately for humanity, Professor John Robinson has developed a hyperdrive that permits faster-than-light travel. Said travel must occur between two hypergates, one at the starting point and one at the destination,

because, as Professor Robinson explains, "If you try to enter hyperspace without a gate, your exit vector is random. There's no telling where you'd come out ... There's a lot of space to get lost in out there."

Getting lost is not something John Robinson is planning to do—it so happens that he and his family are going to make a ten-year journey at sub-light-speed to a planet across the galaxy, where a crew is already at work on a hypergate, the mate to the one being constructed in orbit around the Earth. By the time the Robinsons reach their destination, Alpha Prime, and emerge from the cryo-sleep tubes—a suspended-animation life-support system developed and managed by the oldest Robinson offspring, Dr. Judy Robinson—construction on both hypergates will be completed. Travel between Alpha Prime and Earth will be instantaneous, the human race will be saved and begin to explore the universe.

The Robinson family, all geniuses, have been in training for the mission for the

Meet the new crew, same as the old crew ... with some key differences

Getting ready for the press conference sequence. Hopkins always envisioned each scene in detail before setting it up.

past three years, and they are not a happy bunch. In trying to save humanity, especially his own family, John Robinson has become an all but absent father. The youngest Robinson, Will, turns his school upside down with hacker tricks, trying to get his father's attention. Middle child Penny hates the whole idea and is completely against the mission. "For the last three years I have missed everything, training so I can spend the next ten years missing everything else," she tells her mother, Maureen, on their last night on Earth. Instead of staying home as her mother asks, she sneaks out to say good-bye to her entire life. "Do I spend my last night on Earth watching Mom and Dad pretend not to be fighting again, or blow ten years' worth of allowance at the mall?" she says to her brother as she climbs out the window. "*You* do the math."

And yes, there's a lot of tension between Maureen and John Robinson—the demands of family and career take their toll on both of them. The younger kids are in and out of trouble all the time, and the eldest, Maureen says, has become a ghost, "just like her father." John's protests that he's trying to compensate for a new launch date don't cut much ice with Maureen. "What do you think I'm doing, throwing Tupperware parties?" she asks him.

Nothing is easy; they even have to replace their original pilot at the last minute, with a hotshot hero type who considers the job to be glorified baby–sitting, beneath his talents and skills. But finally *Jupiter 2* lifts off from Houston and everything seems fine . . . briefly. It turns out that there's a saboteur on board, an inadvertent stowaway who, having reprogrammed the construction Robot to destroy the ship sixteen hours into the journey, was himself betrayed by his benefactors, that rendered unconscious so he would perish with the Robinsons.

The saboteur, Zachary Smith, wakes the Robinsons to save his own life, and though Will manages to re-reprogram—deprogram?—the Robot with one of his hacking devices, *Jupiter 2* has gone off course and is about to fall into the sun. The only chance for survival is the hyperdrive. It wasn't meant to be used before they'd reached their destination, but there's no choice. And so, without a hypergate to direct the journey, the bickering Robinsons, their rebellious children, a pilot who thinks of the *Jupiter 2* as an overbuilt RV, and a sneaky, cowardly, and completely untrustworthy prisoner all must face up to the fact that they are lost . . . in space.

Stephen Hopkins was always in the midst of the action

An interplanetary coffee break while Gary Oldman and Stephen Hopkins talk over Dr. Smith's next bit of villainy.

And then, things *really* start to get interesting . . .

Update *Lost in Space?* There seemed to have been two schools of thought on that matter: (1) Are you crazy? and (2) Why not? Many people would argue that the appeal of *Lost In Space* was always in the shaky sets, the sixties-style space costumes, the funky aliens and monsters, Dr. Smith's various signature lines, from "Oh, the pain . . . the pain" to "Never fear—Smith is here" to the high, wordless scream that was his inevitable reaction to any threat. And, of course, a very helpful robot whose sensors could detect aliens in the area and who would call out, very helpfully, "Danger! Danger! Alien lifeform approaching!" Or the more familiar, "Danger, Will Robinson, danger!"

For Akiva Goldsman, who served both as scriptwriter and producer for the

updated *Lost In Space*, the appeal was the family. Goldsman remembers growing up in the sixties as a turbulent time in America, and a television show about the cohesion of family touched him on a fundamental level. A protective father, a nurturing mom, siblings who looked out for each other—wearing cool spacesuits, carrying ray guns, and, as Goldsman put it, "fighting the monsters outside, thereby avoiding the monsters inside . . . I loved that." When Richard Saperstein, the executive vice-president of New Line Cinema, proposed that Goldsman write an updated version for the big screen, those were the elements that sparked his imagination.

In reviewing the old TV show, however, Goldsman realized that many people, including those at New Line, might think of *Lost In Space* only in terms of campiness, whereas he felt the real strength of *Lost In Space* was in its heartfelt quality. The show had originally been conceived as fairly straightforward, smart science fiction. Goldsman decided to return *Lost In Space* to its roots. "I had to find that

It takes a lot of people behind the scenes to make a big movie, but they're not alway's busy.

which I think made it compelling to generations of kids, and translate that into a nineties movie venue."

Goldsman and Saperstein talked with several directors who were interested in the project, and in the end they chose Stephen Hopkins, whose previous credits include *Predator 2*, *Nightmare on Elm Street 5*, and *The Ghost and the Darkness*. His enthusiasm for the film as well as his talent for innovative visualization, impressed them. Hopkins himself felt that the script was an interesting mixture of dark and light elements, a sophisticated film that dealt with real issues but was also a science fiction adventure movie that kids and adults could enjoy. The fact that it was a family in space was something Hopkins felt made it completely different from other science fiction films.

Lost In Space with a straight face, Goldsman and Hopkins agreed, called for serious casting. They went directly for high caliber talent, deciding to cast the

Dr. Smith in sabotage mode, unaware that his employers plan to send him into oblivion along with the Robinsons.

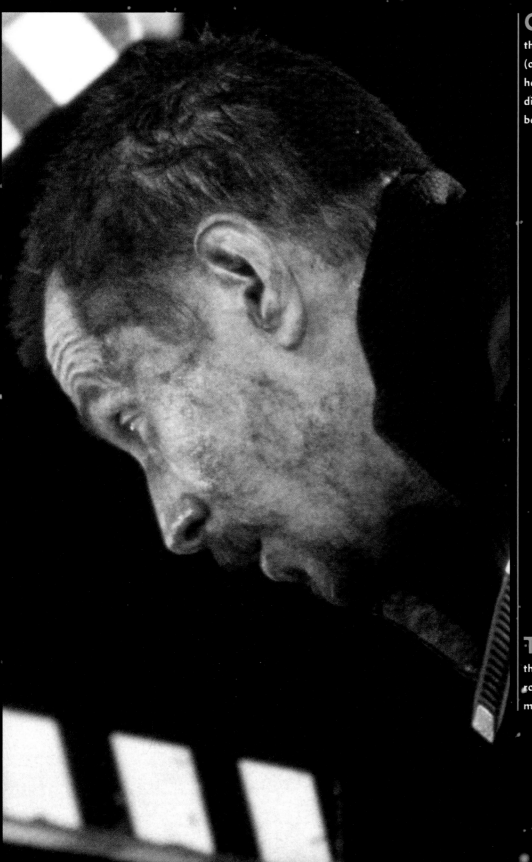

Oldman takes a look
through the lens;
(opposite page, top)
he had just completed
directing *Nil By Mouth*
before *Lost in Space*.

The villain can be
the most interesting
role, but also the
most strenuous.

Dr. Smith on the J2 after the crash-landing on the planet.

Early sketch for Dr. Smith's costume.

part of Dr. Smith first. Several fine actors were mentioned, but in the end they were fortunate enough to get their first choice for the role: Gary Oldman.

For those fans of shrieking, cowardly, Dr. Zachary Smith, who achieved an unequaled level of eloquence when insulting the robot, Gary Oldman seems, well, an unusual casting decision, to say the least. His debut performance as Sid Vicious in *Sid and Nancy* was startlingly authentic; his next major role, as playwright Joe Orton in *Prick Up Your Ears*, was completely different and no less authentic. Since then he has been, among other things, an attorney who frees a mur-

Rescuing Judy, after cutting a deal with Maureen for her daughter's life. Dr. Smith always follows his own best interests . . . *only.*

Lost in Space takes shape under Stephen Hopkins's enthusiasm and Gary Oldman's intensity.

derer, an Irish-American gangster, Lee Harvey Oswald, Dracula, corrupt cops, a white Rastafarian pimp with delusions of blackness, and a future-world villain with a partly plastic skull. Oldman's credentials as a serious actor have been solid from the beginning. Casting him in this role made it clear that, with all due respect, this would be no Jonathan Harris impersonation—this Dr. Smith would be much more treacherous, and thus more dangerous.

In reading the script, Gary Oldman knew that it would be a departure from the old TV show and a departure from standard science fiction movies with lots of explosions and various spacecraft whizzing through the void shooting beams of colored light at each other. Not that the film would be short on special effects. Oldman himself ended up figuring prominently in some that are a first for any feature film to date. But more than anything, he was intrigued by Stephen Hopkins's particular vision of *Lost In Space*, from

William Hurt—
nothing is easy for this
John Robinson.

John Robinson, now
literally isolated in his
cryotube.

the family dynamic to the broader picture
of a depleted future Earth, so much so
that he overcame any reluctance he might
have had to playing yet another villain in
what was becoming a long series.

Hopkins and Goldsman continued
casting in the belief that the movie would
work only with actors capable of present-
ing themselves as real people in extraordinary situations. The more fantastic the
setting, the greater the need for genuine
emotional resonance in the crises. Only
great actors, Goldsman believed, could
portray these dysfunctional, fallible,

totally human people adrift in a hostile universe well enough to make an audience not only accept the situations on the screen, but care about them, and even relate them to their own experiences.

This would seem to make William Hurt a most sincere choice for John Robinson, in the best sense of that word. The part of a brilliant scientist, who is also a concerned father, trying to save the human race simply for the love of his family and who is, paradoxically, taken away from his family by these obligations, would seem to be well-suited to the actor who made his debut as the hero in *Altered States*—a man who was also a loving husband and father and risked the unknown in search of something better, and who nearly lost everyone he loved because of it.

Hurt brings a thoughtfulness and intensity to the role of John Robinson, as well as the conviction that relationships are more important than the pyrotechnics of special effects. In Hurt's view, John Robinson is a man who believes that saving his family—which is to say, not only his immediate family, but the entire human race that is everyone's family—will provide greater stimulation for his genius-level intellect than going to war with hostile forces would. Ultimately, as Hurt sees it, John Robinson works within the system of his future Earth in order to surpass it rather than succeed as part of it. At the same time, the attempt to save his family also means risking the loss of his family. The fact that these moral and ethical questions aren't easily answered, if they can even be answered at all, is one element that drew Hurt to the part. The prospect of becoming an action figure as well was a source of bemusement for him. "I cannot imagine," he stated at a press conference, "why anyone would want to buy a doll of me." No doubt John Robinson would feel the same.

John Robinson, trying to save humanity without losing his family.

John Robinson trying to work out yet another problem. This shot is another example of the simple made complex by the need to add effects through the windows in the background.

Front view (left) Maureen Robinson in cryo suit. Rear view (Far right) Maureen Robinson in cryo suit.

The updating of *LIS* probably shows most strongly in the women characters. The old series' portrayals reflect the time in which the show was made. Yes, the Maureen Tomlinson Robinson of TV was, in fact, a genius and a scientist with a masters degree in chemical engineering and a doctorate in biochemistry; it made her a great cook after the *Jupiter 2* crash-landed on various planets. In one episode, she even managed to engage in a little computer hacking that resulted in the production of a genuine cherry pie, much to Judy's delight.

Mimi Rogers's Maureen doesn't prepare one single meal onscreen, and is seen near a dinner table only once, the unsuccessful last-night-on-Earth dinner at home in Houston. She is a xenobiologist as well as an environmental biologist and faces the challenges familiar to any mother trying to deal with professional issues, family worries, and her own personal demons.

At first dubious, Rogers was enthusiastic after reading the script—the real people and their real problems at the center of a wild science fiction adventure movie with even more than the usual special effects bells-and-whistles was something she felt would appeal to moviegoers in a big way. It certainly appealed to her.

Rogers brings great strength and presence to the role of Maureen Robinson, but also an emotional vulnerability that any mother—any *parent*—can relate to. She has to be strong for her children, but at the same time she aches for them, feeling their pain and frustration, which adds to her own. By turns nurturing, nononsense, brave, and terrified, this is a Maureen shaped by elements that all working mothers will recognize. Mimi Rogers has played parents before, of many different kinds, from the cheerful and frank working-class lady in Steve Buscemi's *Trees Lounge* to the desperate, tragic lost soul in *The Rapture*. She felt Maureen Robinson was perfect for her.

Maureen tends to Judy (upper left) after the malfunction of her cryotube. The resident M.D. has become the first patient.

Mimi Rogers—she understood Maureen Robinson (lower left) as any other working mother.

Maureen (above, top) in cryo sleep.

Mimi Rogers (above, bottom) —the appeal for her was the fact that the wild science fiction story was rooted in a family situation people could relate to.

If Maureen Robinson is different, Judy Robinson is *Different*, with a capital D. D as in "Doctor," as in "Dr. Judy Robinson to you, Major West." One of the fluffier episodes of the old TV series involved a contest for best go-go girl in the universe. If such a group were to show up now, Dr. Judy Robinson would give them a stare so cold they would fall into cryo sleep without benefit of the freezing pods that she developed for the Robinsons' ten-year journey across the galaxy.

As Heather Graham sees her, Judy is the child who is most similar to her father, John. She, too, is wrapped up in science and technology and driven in her desire to use them to help humanity survive. And, like her father, her relationship with her family suffers because of it. As for any other relationships she might have had outside the family—well, one might imagine her enjoying a professional meeting of the minds with colleagues, but her reaction to fighter-pilot hotshot Don West is to make sure he knows she isn't impressed by his war-hero status, his good looks, or his cocky attitude.

Graham was unfamiliar with the old series when she took the part of Judy. What had attracted her was the very human family story within the big special effects action-adventure movie. As Graham plays her, Judy's character develops along those same lines—the cold, brainy doctor whose life has revolved mostly around science and technology, and who, during the mission to save the Earth, rediscovers her family and realizes how much she loves them. She also discovers that Don West isn't such a bad guy after all, but, being the Judy Robinson that she is, she doesn't stop prodding him or giving him a hard time.

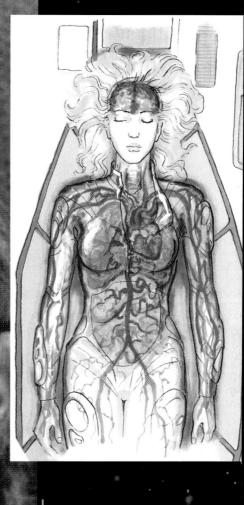

Pre-production concept (above) for bioscan of Judy Robinson.

The film crew (lower left) make a few adjustments for the start of the exploration sequences.

In cryo, (left) the system that Judy Robinson developed for the J2 mission.

Judy (top left) bracing for another rough ride.

Cryotube malfunction (opposite page) creates a striking visual

Judy's brush with death requires a brush with makeup.

Judy takes aim (center) at an unexpected deep space menace.

Judy's portrayal is one more unusual and potent woman in the career of an actress who can show strong presence, even as a doomed drug-user in Gus Van Sant's *Drugstore Cowboy*. Judy Robinson is anything but doomed, of course; Graham gives her a resilient, adventurous quality as well as intelligence and attitude, admitting that she was drawn to *Lost In Space* not only by the opportunity to work with other actors she admired, but out of the urge to try something new.

Heather Graham— *Lost in Space* was a new kind of filmmaking experience for her.

Being a genius doesn't necessarily mean you *want* to save the world, however. If everyone in your family were absorbed in a mission that meant you had to kiss your life good-bye, probably forever—and you were only fourteen years old—you might well decide to sneak out and, as Penny Robinson says, "Blow ten years' worth of allowance at the mall."

Lacey Chabert, a young actress best known for her role as Claudia in the TV series *Party of Five*, found herself completely sympathetic to Penny's point of view. Moviegoers themselves will probably view Penny's reactions to everything as being closer to what their own would be, at least the way Chabert is playing her. Chabert believes there's a little bit of Penny in everyone, even people who don't rebel against their circumstances the way Penny does against hers.

At fourteen, Chabert is the same age as her character, which not only eliminates the need to "play young" but gives her that much more insight into Penny's motivations. For Chabert, Penny is com-

Lacey Chabert: (far left, top) "Character is who you are when nobody else is looking. That definitely applies to Penny!"

Even in the midst of action (center) the camera needs to be carefully contfigured.

The homesickness for Earth (far left, bottom) that Penny shares with Will brings them closer together.

Penny and Blawp, both feeling alone and in need of comfort.

pletely believable—certain features of being an adolescent and a middle child will never change, for as long as humanity survives.

Not that humanity's survival is terribly important to Penny; in a family where high intelligence, science, and technology are prized seemingly more than the family itself—at least by her father, who is all but a stranger to her—Penny rebels by making her concerns completely different. She throws herself into whatever is trendy, following the latest fashions, taking *Vogue* as seriously as the rest of the family take their particular scientific specialties. And if John Robinson and older daughter Judy are too cold and brainy, Penny is the polar opposite: emotional, but trying to hide it behind a façade of what a teenage girl thinks is brittle sophistication, so that no one will know how vulnerable she actually feels. The diary/journal she keeps of her adventures as "Penny Robinson, Space Captive" and her crush on Don West are things that anyone who has ever been to high school will recognize, from the class of 1952 to the class of 2002. Penny's turmoil over starting to grow up and having to give up everything she's known will probably be familiar to anyone whose family had to move for the sake of a parent's career.

Careful rigging (top left) before the lift.

Which way is up?(top center)

Note where set background ends. (bottom left)

Just hanging around the set. (bottom center)

Lacey Chabert: (right) "Penny would like to run to her mom's arms and be cradled, but she can't. She tries to be brave."

Preparing Will to
rebuild the Robot. In
real life, Jack Johnson
was building a robot
when he was cast.

Jack Johnson—what
he liked best about the
character Will was Will's
interest in everything,
and his intelligence.

Will (opposite page,
left) tries to control
the Robot with his
hacker deck.

Danger Will Robinson! is one of those classic lines that just about everyone can quote, or so it seems. Even the Lost In Space movie website could be found at www.dangerwillrobinson.com, which made it one of the easiest web addresses to remember. The character of Will Robinson was practically an archetype, a good boy with a big brain and cute freckles, a kid who would never deliberately go looking for trouble but just couldn't help it if trouble found him, and could always depend on guidance from his dad.

Will Robinson mark 1998 is still a good boy . . . mostly. The big brain that can be turned to the service of saving humanity hacks into the school's power grid to run his science fair experiment, leaving them without lights. When the principal confers, by holographic projection, with his mother over this latest bit of mischief, Will runs a few experiments with the principal's holographic image more for his own entertainment than out of any scientific curiosity.

The youngest actor in the cast, Jack Johnson imbues Will Robinson with a high level of energy, which leads not only to the various ways of acting-out to try to get his father's attention, but to some serious heroics that get everyone's attention at one time or another—literally. But there are also reminders that the boy with the big brain is exactly that: a boy. Who can't resist teasing his older sister.

Will and the friend he (literally) made.

Matt LeBlanc (top)—Mark Goddard, the original Major West, was delighted. "They got one of the handsomest guys in Hollywood to play me!"

Matt LeBlanc (left center)—yet another longtime fan of the original *LIS* series.

Matt LeBlanc: (bottom left) "The design of the film, from my point of view, is *groovy*—everything's round, there are no right angles."

Don West (inset) in his battle helmet, an effect that requires utmost patience from the actor.

Major West, (opposite page) about to discover that the metal-eating spiders don't mind a bit of meat with their steel.

Major Don West (this page right) in full battle regalia.

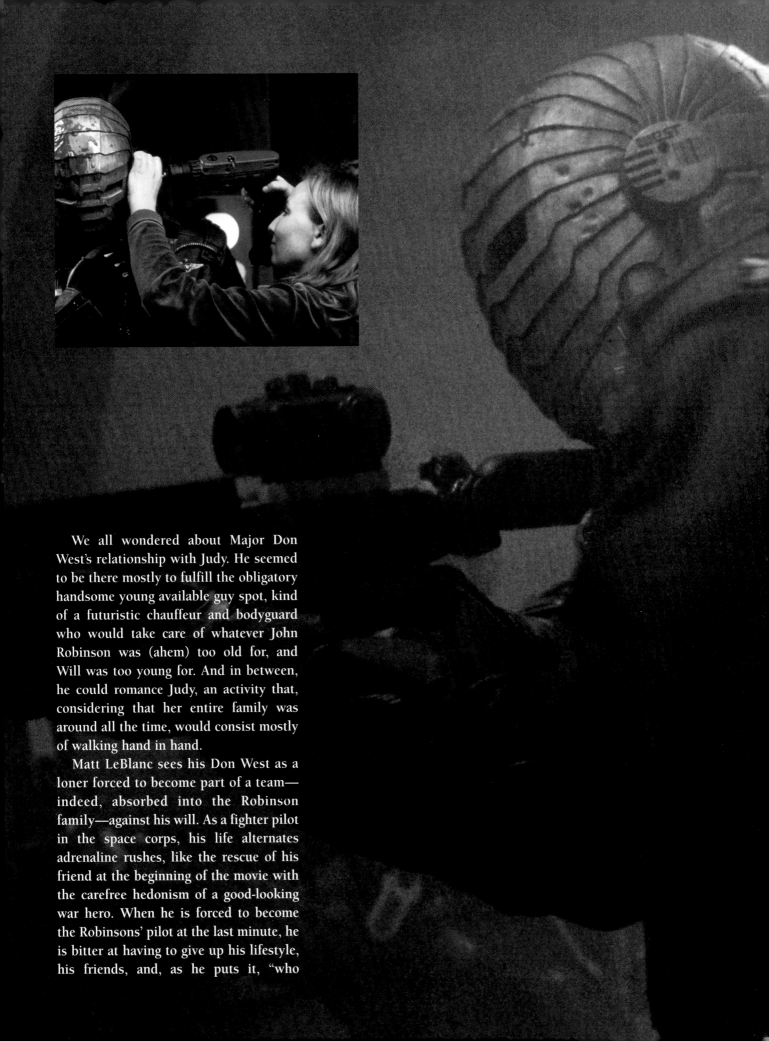

We all wondered about Major Don West's relationship with Judy. He seemed to be there mostly to fulfill the obligatory handsome young available guy spot, kind of a futuristic chauffeur and bodyguard who would take care of whatever John Robinson was (ahem) too old for, and Will was too young for. And in between, he could romance Judy, an activity that, considering that her entire family was around all the time, would consist mostly of walking hand in hand.

Matt LeBlanc sees his Don West as a loner forced to become part of a team—indeed, absorbed into the Robinson family—against his will. As a fighter pilot in the space corps, his life alternates adrenaline rushes, like the rescue of his friend at the beginning of the movie with the carefree hedonism of a good-looking war hero. When he is forced to become the Robinsons' pilot at the last minute, he is bitter at having to give up his lifestyle, his friends, and, as he puts it, "who

Major Don West:
"Never leave your enemy
stronghold intact!"

The impressive *Jupiter 2*
leaves Major West cold.
As far as he's concerned,
it's just a big RV and he's
a babysitter.

"You can get lost
(center) in this world
Stephen has created."

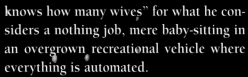

knows how many wives" for what he considers a nothing job, mere baby-sitting in an overgrown recreational vehicle where everything is automated.

Worse, Judy Robinson isn't impressed by his war record or his machismo, two things that always seem to have gotten Don West anything he wanted in the past. But it's a changed Don West who faces an uncertain future, who learns to view women, particularly Judy, quite differently. And, of course, he finds that the Jupiter Mission involves quite a bit more than baby-sitting . . .

Sketch of Don West in cryo suit

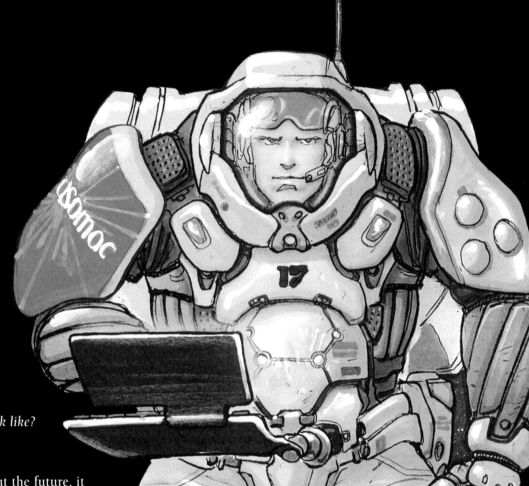

Q. What does the future look like?
A. (1) Like no other future.
  (2) Like it works.

In conceiving a movie about the future, it helps to be visually inclined, which Stephen Hopkins most definitely is, according to everyone who has worked with him. His background includes experience in storyboarding and production design, and work developing rock videos and commercials, before moving on to features like *Predator 2*, *Nightmare on Elm Street 5*, and *The Ghost and the Darkness*.

But there's one other feature in Stephen Hopkins's background that gives him an extra edge visually: he's a comics fan. More than that, he's also an illustrator who has done a few comics himself. So it isn't surprising that he turned to comics for his initial inspiration, encouraging his production designer, Norman Garwood, to do the same.

Norman Garwood's imagination has been described as *wild, frenetic,* even *feverish.* It would have to be—his previous visualizations started with *The Missionary,* moved on to *The Princess Bride* and *Misery,* among others, and then to *Hook, Glory,* and *Brazil,* the three movies for which he received Oscar nominations. In addition, *Brazil* won both the British Academy Award and the London Standard Award, an honor Garwood is particularly proud of. Prior to *LIS,* he had never done a space movie, nor does he actually think of *Brazil* as a science fiction film per se—having worked with Terry Gilliam before, Garwood describes *Brazil* as a Terry Gilliam movie.

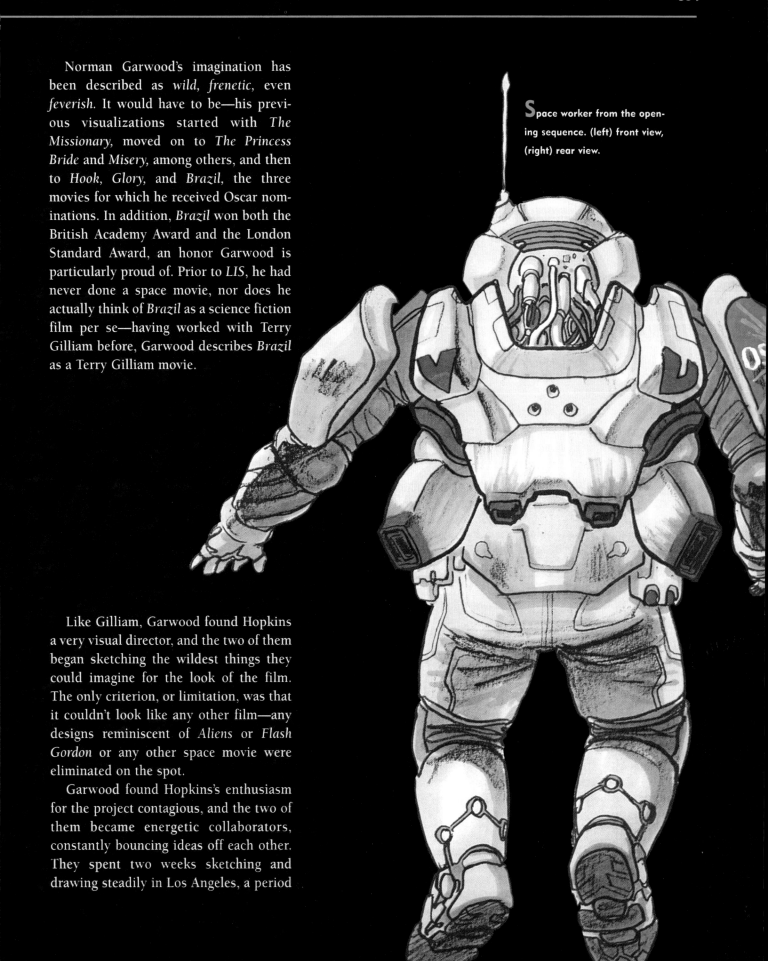

Space worker from the opening sequence. (left) front view, (right) rear view.

Like Gilliam, Garwood found Hopkins a very visual director, and the two of them began sketching the wildest things they could imagine for the look of the film. The only criterion, or limitation, was that it couldn't look like any other film—any designs reminiscent of *Aliens* or *Flash Gordon* or any other space movie were eliminated on the spot.

Garwood found Hopkins's enthusiasm for the project contagious, and the two of them became energetic collaborators, constantly bouncing ideas off each other. They spent two weeks sketching and drawing steadily in Los Angeles, a period

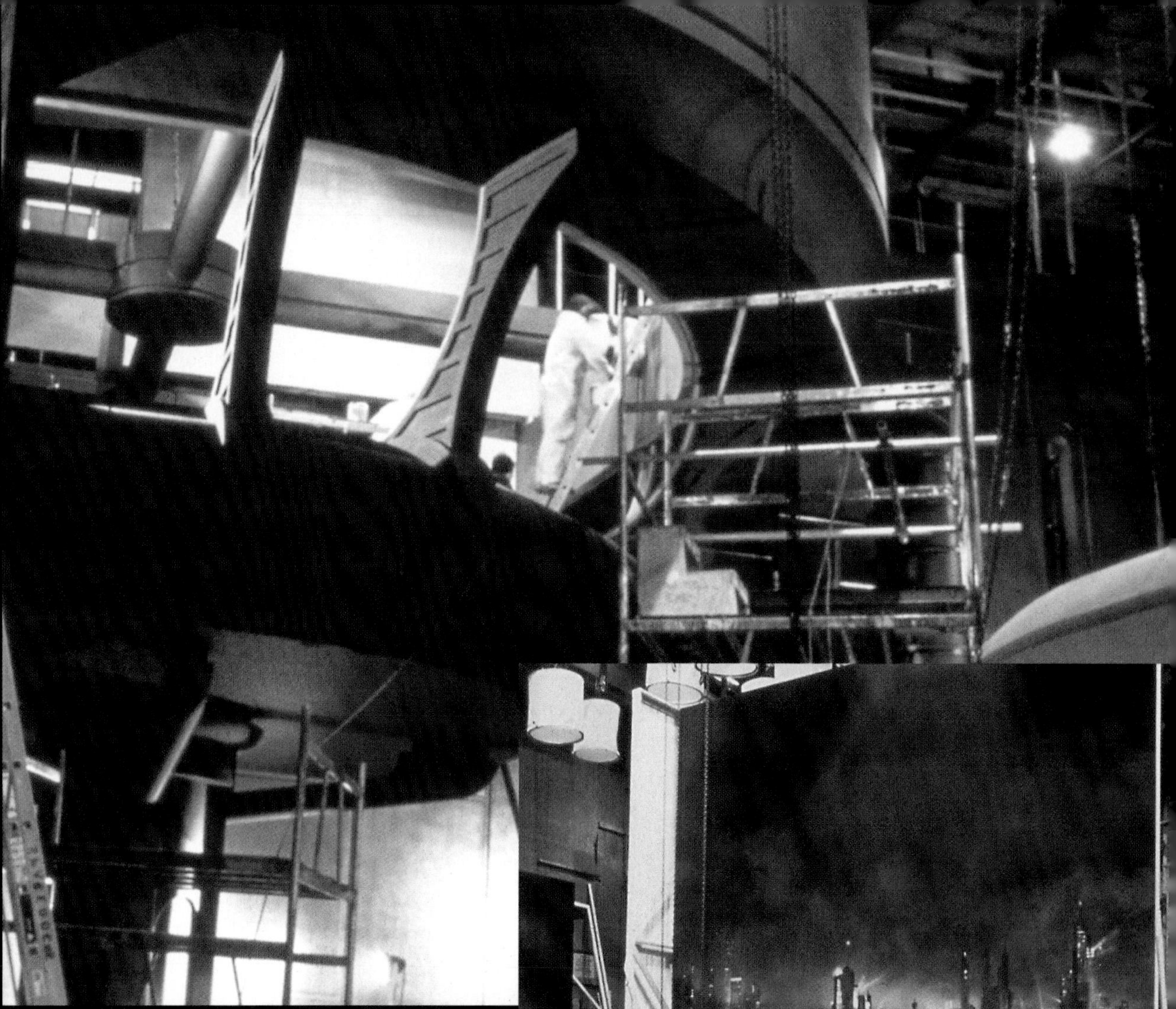

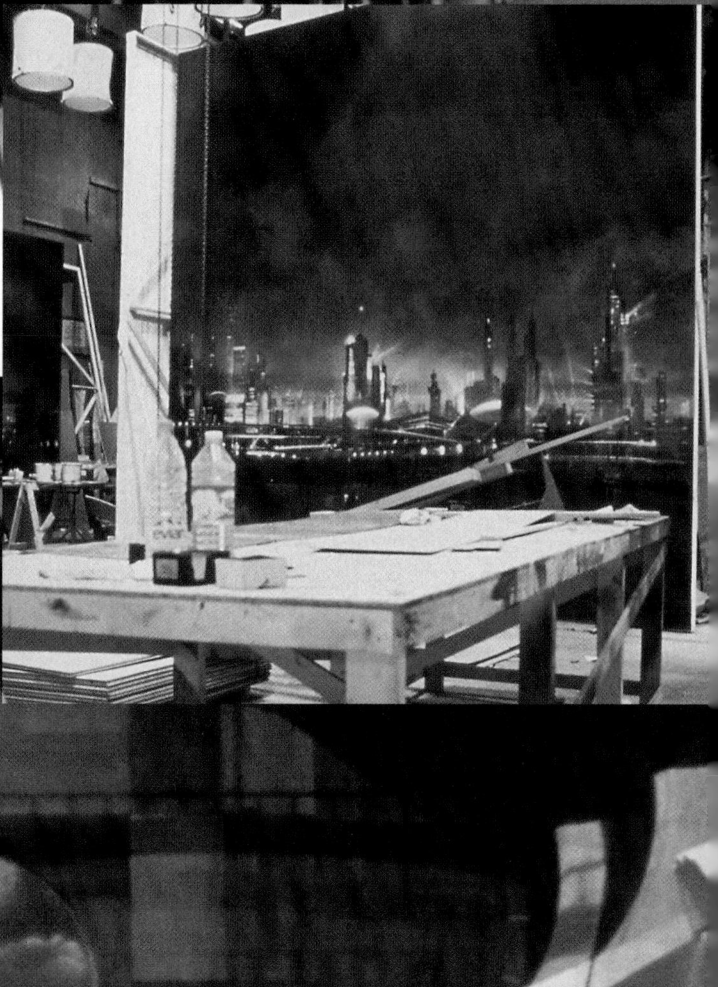

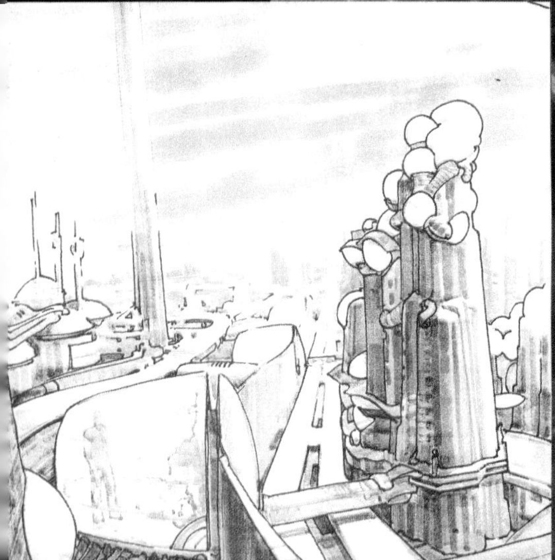

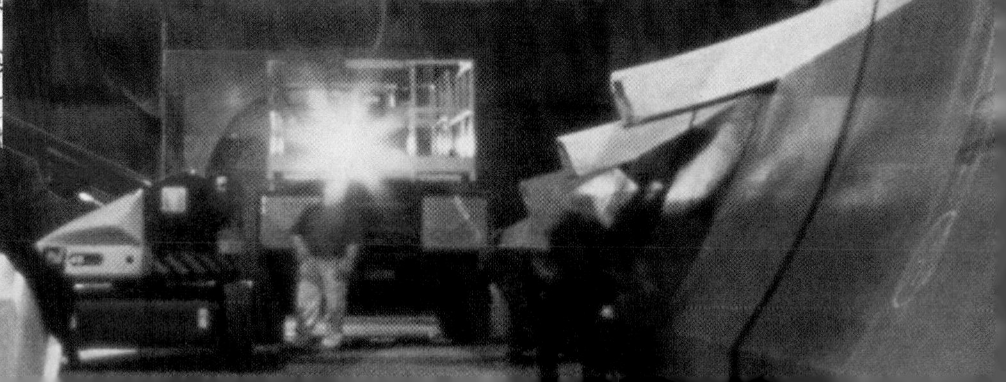

The Houston launch (left) platform was thought out as meticulously as if it had been meant to work for real at full size.

Special effects (bottom left) supervisor Nick Allder: "When I was a kid, I used to have model airplanes and model trains and fireworks. As I got older, I've just gotten bigger toys and bigger fireworks, but basically I'm still a child at heart. It's great!"

Concept sketch (opposite page far left) for future Houston.

The Future, being built (opposite page)—production designer Norman Garwood credited construction manager Malcolm Roberts with making the sets a success. "He's brought together some of the most talented, intelligent people." Note some background art in place to help focus on set creative efforts.

Detail of futuristic technology (upper left)—component of air filtration system in future Houston.

Rough rendering (below) of future Houston with launch tower in background.

Near-final model (left) of lauch tower.

Individualistic highrise tower (inset) buildings create a unique skyline for future Houston.

40

The press conference, inside one of the "comfort domes" that make life on Earth possible. Outside? Don't go there.

that Garwood describes as a very vital, creative time. On occasion, ideas demanding development would wake him at four in the morning and he would tiptoe into the bathroom to sketch them out on hotel stationery, so as not to wake his wife.

Eventually, the look that would be *LIS* began to take shape, and that shape was an egg. The *LIS* look, they decided, would have no straight lines anywhere, something that would give it a more organic look than was usual for space movies. After all, Hopkins reasoned, thirty years ago, in the sixties, everyone had conceived of a future that would be all concrete and plastic, and things hadn't turned out that way; so why not try to present a vision of the future from here that would look unusual, even a bit unexpected, but at the same time functional?

Screen images to be added later, one of over seven hundred effects in total.

The final vision of the future was a collaboration between Stephen Hopkins and Norman Garwood, with a little input from everyone involved.

Norman Garwood: (bottom left) "No matter what kind of set you do, the cameraman can make it or break it." Garwood was delighted to be working with director of photography Peter Levy again.

Stephen Hopkins and Norman Garwood envisioned each set down to the last and most minute details.

In the future there will still be PR. Two pieces of material promoting the *Jupiter* launch.

The multitude of *Lost in Space* fans around the world will recognize a couple of faces in this press conference scene.

There were four general areas to build sets for: prelaunch Earth; the *Jupiter 2*; the *Proteus*, where the Robinsons first encounter aliens; and the alien planet where they crash-land. Aside from the launching of the spacecraft in Houston, there would be some relatively brief scenes in the Robinson home and views of Houston itself as a more or less typical large city on the exhausted, dying Earth, with people living within comfort domes where the air could be filtered, in order to survive. Hopkins wanted to go for fantastic and extraordinary, but at the same time he felt it all needed to be grounded in as realistic a treatment as possible.

Another idea. (right) Which Houston would you like?

The lush look (center) of the greenery is only a facade over a planet choking to death.

Preparing John Robinson's workbench with what every genius scientist father tinkers with at home—a hyperdrive.

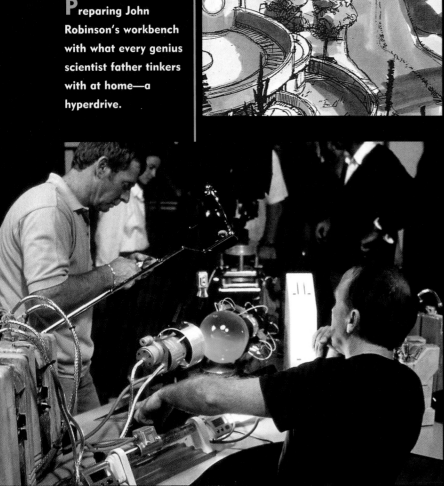

It was this same desire that sent him to NASA to talk seriously with experts there about the dynamics of groups going into space. As it turned out, NASA had been doing family studies themselves, with the idea that a family may be the best configuration for long-range space missions. Perhaps most people, however, wouldn't feel that way—as Hopkins himself stated: "We all have family issues, and everyone's nightmare is Thanksgiving Day, forever and ever and ever. In real life, you'd be stuck in a spaceship with your family whether you like it or not."

This situation could be trying for the most loving of families, something the Robinsons most definitely are not, at least to start with. A real family like the Robinsons made it even more important, in Hopkins's view, that the sets not defy credibility.

For Norman Garwood, this meant paying special attention to the *Jupiter 2* and to

The future (above) will have clutter very much like we do today.

Will Robinson (inset) in his room—thanks to the mission, he'll have to leave most of his stuff behind.

It was important to Norman Garwood (right) that the sets keep the eye interested.

Drawing of the Blawp ship. (bottom)

The Robot's lair (opposite page, top)—ready for a dramatic entrance.

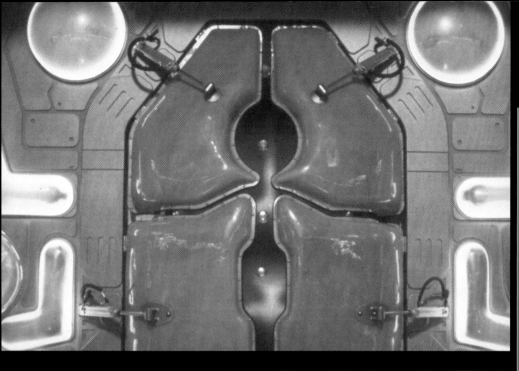

The stairs in the Robinson home probably have the only straight lines to be found in the movie— and even those spiral.

The Robinson home, (bottom) in progress— set decorator Anna Pinnock called the style "avant-garde sixties, rather than nostalgic."

the planet—each presented its own set of problems, both in design and execution.

The *Jupiter 2* evolved from something that almost resembled a jellyfish to a living space that suggests organic origins, almost as if it had been grown rather than built, with a hint of Gothic cathedral about it. But it had to be more than just a backdrop for the actors. The set itself had to shake, physically; the chairs had to rise up and down, there was an elevator platform in part of the floor, the monitors had to do certain things, and there were the cryotubes, which had their own moving parts. All of it had to intrigue the eye and the interest of the moviegoer *and* make sense, *and* function properly for the pur-

On the eve of the launch, (right) John Robinson introduces daughter Dr. Judy Robinson to Major Don West on the J2 bridge. Judy has been prepping the cryotubes.

Looking onto the bridge (opposite page, top left) of the *Jupiter 2*, with the organic-looking navigational system in the center, green screens visible through the windows in the background. Fantastic cosmic scenery to be added later.

poses of the director, the actors, and the special effects. Instead of getting a headache, Hopkins and Garwood got Nick Allder.

Allder grew up on film sets—his father worked for Technicolor building three-strip cameras and Allder spent his summer vacations from school working in small studios. He lit and shot models for TV programs, built his own equipment so he could do pictures underwater, and eventually turned to special effects, winning an Academy Award for the first *Alien* movie. Having known Norman Garwood for many years, and having worked with him before, Allder was able to get right into preparation, a full seven months before actual filming began.

It would take a genius (far left) to put together a robot out of this jumble of spare parts. Fortunately, Will Robinson is one.

Final costume adjustments (left) for the next shot.

Dr. Zachary Smith is making his own pre-flight preparations for the *Jupiter 2*, never thinking that it will all go horribly wrong.

The ground crew (below) prepares the *Jupiter 2* for launch.

Major Don West in his cryo suit, at the navigational system. From this angle, it is easy to see how closely the design of the cryo suit and the bridge are to each other.

Drawing of down angle on hyperdrive.

Early concept drawing
for the cryotube section

Another view (below)
of a cryotube in use

Allder was also of the fantastic-but-functional school of thought regarding the set, the props, and the physical effects. He knew they had to go about building things as if they were really going to see use as whatever they were meant to be, whether it was a prop weapon or a chair on the *Jupiter 2* bridge. Pad and pen in hand, Allder worked closely with both Hopkins and Garwood, determining how much room would be needed to make each thing fit and work, and went on to work just as closely with the construction crew.

Garwood described the lack of straight lines on the *Jupiter 2* set as being a nightmare for construction manager Malcolm Roberts. The chores for Roberts's crew didn't end there, however—there were major engineering concerns about the physical effects that would provide the realism Hopkins was shooting for.

Working from a practical design, the

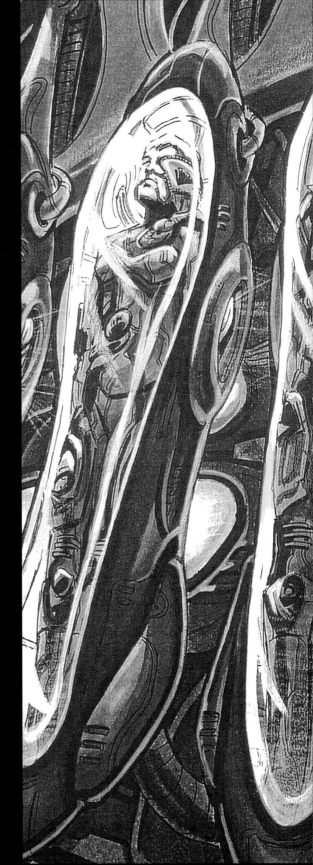

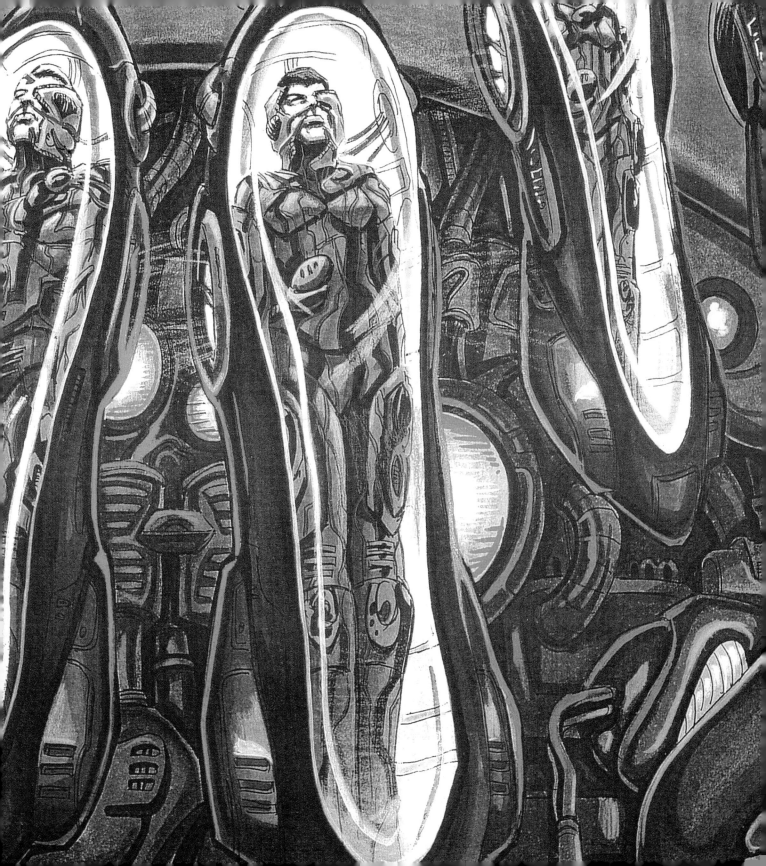

Judy Robinson (Heather Graham) in the complete cryo rig—tube, suit, and eyepiece. Special effects costumer Vin Burnham consulted an intensive care nurse on the placement of life-support devices.

The cryotubes on the *Jupiter 2*. In the joint vision of Stephen Hopkins and Norman Garwood, they were to look more as if they had been grown than manufactured, but it was up to Nick Allder's crew to make them function.

An attempt to show affection before entering cryo sleep, but neither father nor son know quite what to do. John Robinson's work has kept him so absent, this is one of the few times he's tucked Will in.

Setting up one of the cryotube shots.

Freed from the cryotube , Judy still needs extraordinary life-saving measures to survive.

Stephen Hopkins decides on a camera angle for one of many action scenes on the *J2*. Production designer Norman Garwood credits Hopkins's background as a comic illustrator and art director for his intensely visual approach to filmaking

Jack Johnson was proud to do many of his own stunts, thanks to safety-conscious special effects supervisor Nick Allder, who knew exactly how to keep him and the other actors safe.

Dr. Smith's sabotage—the explosions are only the beginning of their troubles.

seats on the bridge had to move not just up and down, but laterally, from one area of the console to the other. There was also a platform lift built into the floor. As well, the entire floor of the *Jupiter*'s bridge, which measured ninety by sixty feet and weighed thirty tons, had to move, shake, and vibrate at various speeds; Allder used a computer to drive the floor, so it could move in any direction and vibrate at any speed necessary. Determining that the platform lift could not be attached to the

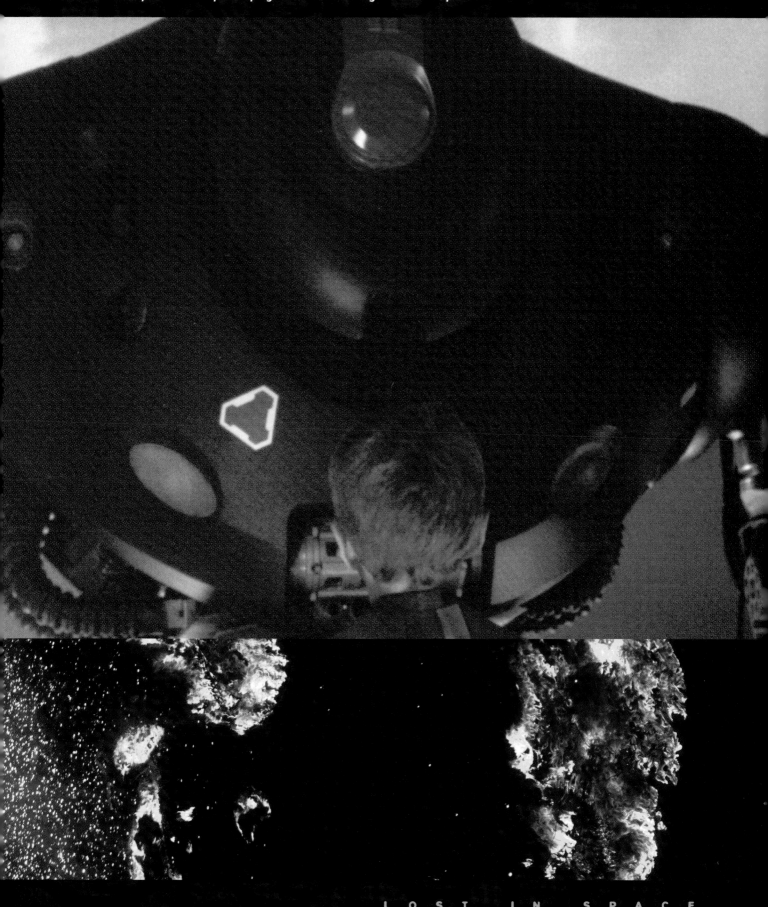

Will and the first robot coming up to the J2 bridge on the platform elevator. Nick Allder had to lower the platform and put a "plug" in the hole during the crash sequences.

57

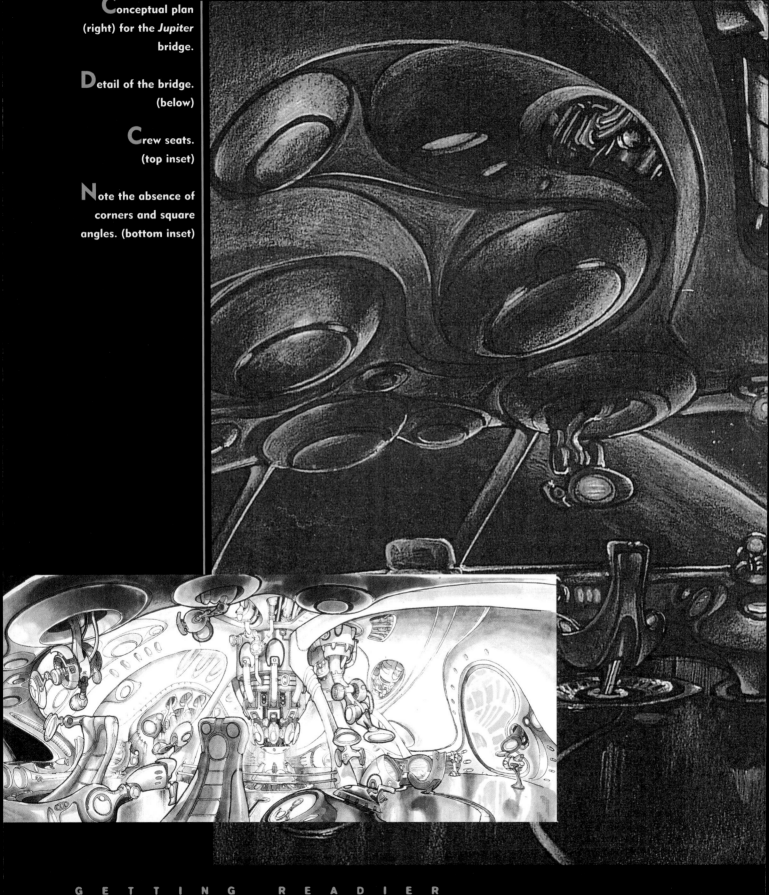

Conceptual plan (right) for the *Jupiter* bridge.

Detail of the bridge. (below)

Crew seats. (top inset)

Note the absence of corners and square angles. (bottom inset)

that these were functional and practical pieces of equipment had to be inherent in the designs. Anything made to be functional had to develop. "That's why a real weapon works," Allder says. "You don't design it and say, 'This is what it's going to look like.' You work it from the beginning. Like a car, which starts off with four wheels and a gear box. Once you've got the basic shape, everything falls into place. That's why machines look like the right-looking thing—they evolve through manufacturing. That determines how they're designed." Allder and his team took blocks of metal and machined pieces to make it practical. Knowing that electronics had to be fitted inside, they worked with the weapons, machining away some parts and fitting on others, until they came up with the final prop.

One of Allder's special accomplishments, however, was Don West's bubble-fighter, which he saw not just as a piece of equipment, but an essential element in establishing West's character as a heroic fighter-pilot. What he came up with, working from Norman Garwood's designs, was a big Perspex bubble with a seat inside; the controls would be on the pilot's arms. These controls would govern the motion of the bubble in such a way that the fighter would operate much like an extension of the pilot's body—a spacecraft that pilots do not climb into so much as put on

Penny (Lacey Chabert): "On the bridge, when we're staring out at blast shields, we're looking at a green screen or a little arrow on a stick, which somebody carries across." Thanks to computer-generated special effects, moviegoers see something entirely different.

top of the floor when the floor was moving, Allder fitted a special top piece to level the floor while the lift was lowered out of the way.

Practicality would probably be the keyword for Nick Allder and his team, which at one point grew to twenty-six people spread over two units and four soundstages—that, or *functional.* From the beginning, he was most concerned that whatever he worked on, whether it was the floor of the spacecraft or the hand-held weapons used by the actors, the idea

Stephen Hopkins explains to his actors (opposite page) what they're supposed to be seeing through the windows. Lacey Chabert (Penny) said Hopkins was very good at describing how things would eventually look.

Another view of the bridge chairs in action. (lower right)

Major Don West in the versatile bridge chairs, which rise up eighteen feet. They were built to move from side to side as well.

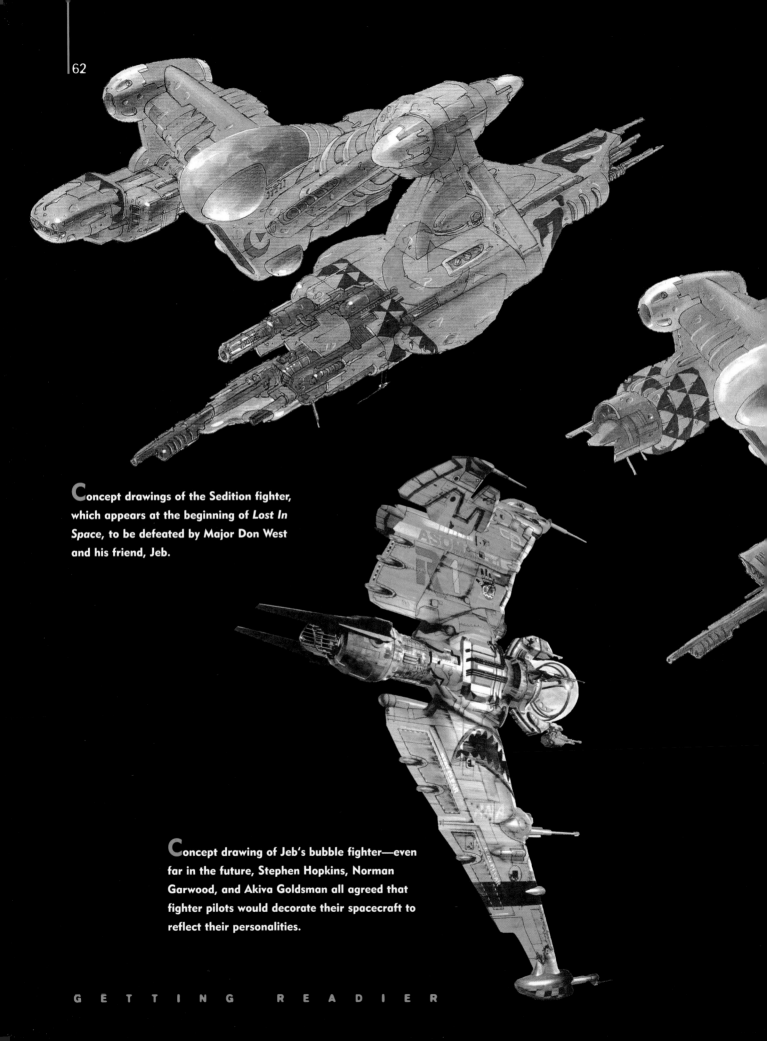

Concept drawings of the Sedition fighter, which appears at the beginning of *Lost In Space*, to be defeated by Major Don West and his friend, Jeb.

Concept drawing of Jeb's bubble fighter—even far in the future, Stephen Hopkins, Norman Garwood, and Akiva Goldsman all agreed that fighter pilots would decorate their spacecraft to reflect their personalities.

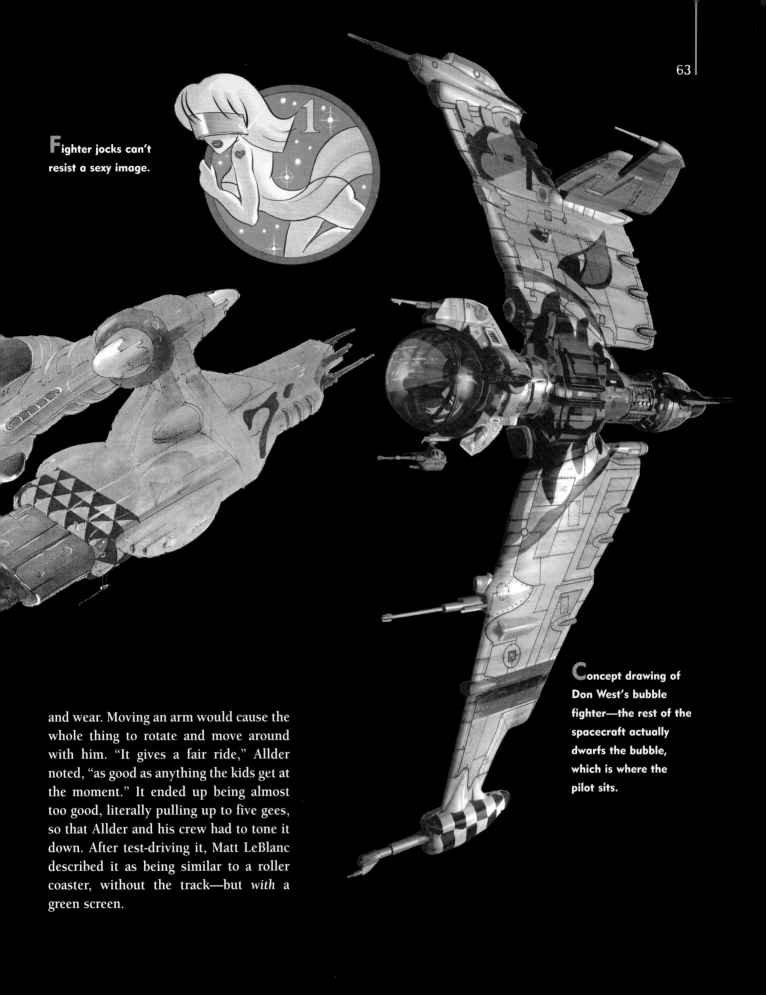

Fighter jocks can't resist a sexy image.

Concept drawing of Don West's bubble fighter—the rest of the spacecraft actually dwarfs the bubble, which is where the pilot sits.

and wear. Moving an arm would cause the whole thing to rotate and move around with him. "It gives a fair ride," Allder noted, "as good as anything the kids get at the moment." It ended up being almost too good, literally pulling up to five gees, so that Allder and his crew had to tone it down. After test-driving it, Matt LeBlanc described it as being similar to a roller coaster, without the track—but *with* a green screen.

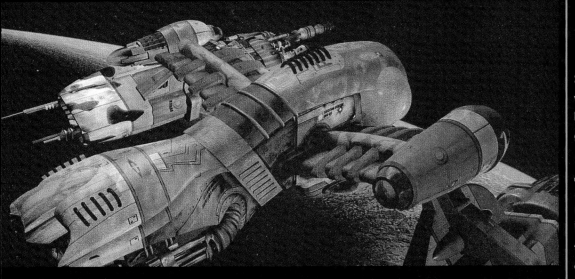

Drawing of the Sedition raider (left) with the planetary horizon in the background.

This shot of Major Don West (Matt LeBlanc) shows that the bubble seating area was actually the only part of the bubble fighter that existed outside the computer.

Major Don West demonstrates his ability to remain cool under pressure.

Jeb in his bubble fighter—none of the equipment is extraneous or just for show. The controls on the actor's arms actually moved the seat in whatever direction he gestured, which meant being careful about making any sudden motions.

That was the catch: like so many other elements to come in *LIS*, the bubble fighter was only partially in existence. That is, the only elements of Don West's and Jeb's fighter craft that had any reality outside of a computer were the actors and the bubble they were strapped into. Sequences were shot against green screens, in preparation for the compositing that would take place in postproduction.

Not that this made Nick Allder's job any easier. From the design stage to the finish, the bubble fighter alone took eleven weeks to construct, including the time Allder used to have an independent company double-check the stress and strain factors. In the end it was very much like building an actual aircraft, since the same safety procedures had to be followed.

Safety is the biggest reason why all sequences involving physical effects are carefully choreographed. Nothing could be left to chance; Allder and his crew had to know where everyone was going to be at a given time and to watch carefully. With so much going on, an actor could miss his spot or get too close to something hazardous. In Allder's view, it's always better not to have some pyrotechnic or other effect go off than to risk hurting someone, and with so many hydraulic rigs on the set, no one wanted to take a chance of anyone getting crushed.

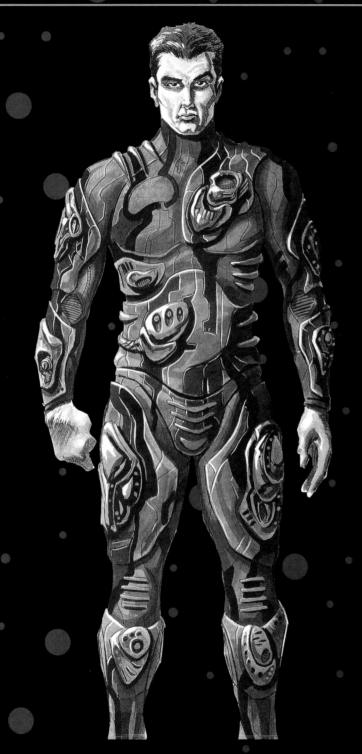

clothing for the sequences on Earth, Burnham went to work on what she calls special effects costuming, outfits such as the cryo suits, which had to serve not only as clothing but as life-support equipment for the wearers while in their cryotubes.

Burnham would seem to be the ideal choice for this kind of task. After a decade in live theater, where she started out constructing props and moved on to pantomime horses, ballet headdresses, and what she describes as "endless mice for *The Nutcracker Suite*," she progressed to designing small but very difficult pieces for commercials. Eventually, she designed the special costumes for the two Tim Burton *Batman* movies: Batman, Catwoman, and the Penguin.

Time was short when she went to work on *Lost in Space*, and there was little or no time to experiment and change things. The key to costuming in her specialized area, Burnham says, is the director and what he has in mind, how he sees the characters. Often, special effects costumes have been conceived before the actors even start rehearsing, and it was so in this case, particularly with the cryo suits, which involved a lot of foam and took a long time to construct. Burnham had some ideas as to how the characters should look, and the actors had their own ideas, too. The teamwork among all of them meant the costumes developed and evolved, with input from several sources instead of just one or two.

Burnham turned some of the components of the cryo suits over to model-maker Colin Campbell, who decided to use optic fibers and LEDs for the costume parts that lit up. Burnham found the blue

So, what *does* the well-dressed modern family wear while lost in space? Stephen Hopkins and Norman Garwood knew that if anyone could answer that question, it would be Vin Burnham. While Robert Bell and Gilly Hebden handled the design of futuristic

LEDs in Los Angeles after spotting them on Mr. Freeze's costume during the filming of *Batman Forever* (coincidentally written by Akiva Goldsman). Campbell worked out how to use purple ones as well. But Burnham emphasized that the wiring-up for LEDs was not the thing that made them special effects costumes.

"It's the sculpting and molding process," she says, describing the molding as being similar to baking a cake. Specialized mold-makers had to make very exact molds, which specialized foam technicians injected with foam and baked in an oven. Any foam that came out of a mold with bubbles on the surface was unacceptable, and the failure rate for the molds was very high. But there was no better way of producing the necessary costume pieces.

Special effects costuming, Burnham says, was like prosthetic makeup, prosthetics for the body. "It's done in the same way. When we made Catwoman's costume, we used a life-cast of Michelle Pfeiffer and sculpted clay over the head, so the headpiece fitted exactly. The clay that we used for *Lost in Space* is used to sculpt prototypes for cars. We were trying to tie the costumes in with the *Jupiter 2*, so they had a machinelike quality, which is one of the things that Stephen wanted to get."

The time crunch, however, meant there was precious little opportunity to put her head together with Hopkins and Garwood. Garwood was busy designing the sets while Burnham worked on the costumes, and she did her best to take a lot of the costumes' lines from the spaceship design. Philippe Stark's designs provided inspiration as well.

Burnham wanted to go for as much originality as possible, but at the same time, she admits, "everything's been done. And you're restricted—you've got a *human* body. That human body has got to

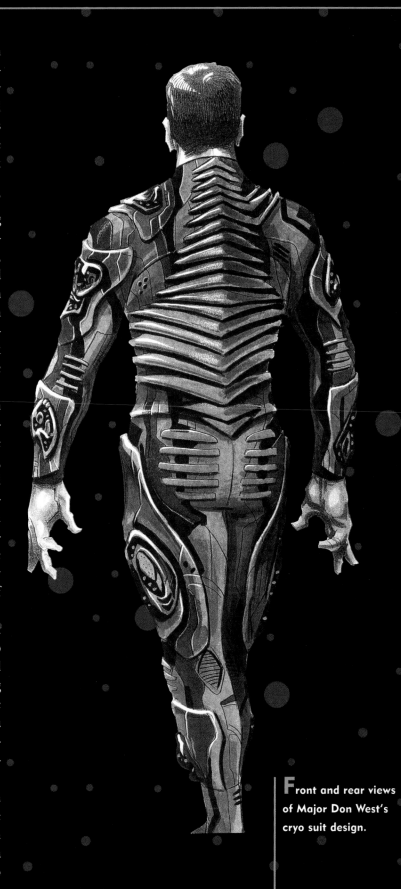

Front and rear views of Major Don West's cryo suit design.

be able to get in and out of the costume, the actors have to be able to move when they're in it, it's got to be reasonably comfortable." Her solution to this was to approach the costumes as if she were making them for dancers, keeping all of the joints completely clear.

Even so, the cryo suits were hot, heavy, and tight. "There's a sort of costume technology that you have to keep up with," Burnham noted, "and it changes all the time. Audiences expect things that are sophisticated, Lycra all-over suits are no longer acceptable." Burnham compared making the cryo suits to making a prototype of a car, in that they had to have a certain kind of finish to them.

Making the camera love the costumes,

or, indeed, making certain finishes look like what they were *not*—such as parts that needed to look like metal and not molded foam—meant testing surfaces and paint finishes under various kinds of lighting, and that meant having the physical object itself, not just a picture.

Burnham hit on an interference color for parts of the cryo suits, a blue that changes a certain amount under light, which complicated things to some extent, as there was quite a lot of blue and green screen in the production for the sake of special effects which would be added in postproduction. So after getting the okays from the lighting camera staffs, Burnham had to keep checking with Angus Bickerton, who was handling the special visual effects, to make sure the blues she chose wouldn't create problems later.

The technical side of creating the costumes dwarfed the artistic in every way. The cryo suits had to be made to the exact specifications of each actor's body, which meant that head-to-toe life-casts of the actors had to be made. This involved each actor standing encased in plaster for two hours, an ordeal under any circumstances, but especially when an actor had to somehow squeeze the time into an already-busy schedule. Heather Graham had to make a special overnight trip from New York, where she was shooting something else, to the Henson Creature Shop in Los Angeles where the life-casting was taking place.

The typical procedure for life-casting is to coat the actor, wearing as little as possible, in Vaseline, the release agent between flesh and plaster. A team of four experienced mold-makers cover the actor from head to foot in plaster and then prop him/her up on a wooden frame while the plaster hardens—not the sort of thing you'd want to undergo if you're even the least bit claustrophobic. Burnham had nothing but praise for all the actors, who handled the ordeal extremely well.

Even so, there were problems. One actor's set of costumes turned out too tight,

and Jack Johnson (Will) actually grew two and a half inches between the life-casting and the costume fitting. Since it was necessary to make eight cryo suits for each actor, this meant making a total of twenty-four for Jack alone. Meanwhile, Lacey Chabert (Penny) *lost* weight. All these technical difficulties required not only specialized costumers to keep everything going, but very patient actors as well.

Four sculptors worked on the costume designs, carefully considering every aspect of the human body. Burnham also made use of the talents of Max Goodrich, who worked on the design for the new London taxi. "He makes these beautiful little models of cars that are immaculate," Burnham says. "We needed that finish, that machine-like finish that he got from his sculpting. He had a huge input to training the others in using that particular kind of clay that is like carving in stone, the clay is so hard. You have to heat it in the microwave to use it. Everybody on the team is key. The sculptors were all extremely good sculptors. The mold-makers included Kelly Wilson, who is well-known for doing the best bodycasts and molds for foam. He handled all of the mold-making. That was one reason I wanted to set up at Henson's, to get the facility of their mold shop, which is the best. Tahra Kharibian and Jeeda Barfoot, they were like two right hands—assistant designers, organizers, buyers—found people to do things, they found amazing materials, and kept the workshop running."

Ever mindful of details, Burnham also consulted an intensive-care nurse about the placement of the specially molded foam cryo-plates, which were to function not merely as futuristic decoration, but as part of the life-support system. "They're basically sensors that connect to people in the cryotubes, they're designed to keep them alive," Burnham says. "You have to get away from things being purely decorative. Most machines look wonderful, but they were designed to *look* wonderful, they

Major Don West's fantastic battle helmet (upper left) —its appearance on the *Proteus* is actually a stop-motion special effect, where each panel of the helmet is added one at a time and then filmed, with sound added later.

The J2 crew coming out of cryo sleep to save Dr. Smith (center) from his own sabotage, and, not incidentally, to save themselves. The LEDs (visible on John's cryo suit) meant adding a battery pack to the actor's suit.

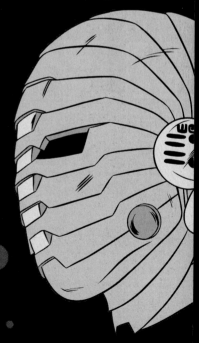

Spiders beware. (lower left)

were designed to function. One thing Stephen was concerned about was that these things look like they could *work*. So I designed them for certain areas, and then I called in this intensive-care nurse and said, 'What do you think in this context—is this ridiculous? When people like you are watching the film, are you just going to laugh and say, 'How could anyone think this would work?' He said no and showed us a lot of rather grisly pictures of people in intensive care with monitors and equipment. None of it is quite as exciting-looking as the cryos, so there's a bit of artistic license there. But he did say that it was all actually feasible, that they could have those monitors in those places. So intensive care at Charing Cross Hospital will vouch for us!"

Burnham was in Los Angeles for three weeks in the beginning, which was quite difficult, as Kharibian and Barfoot were making prototypes and mock-ups in London. Burnham found herself faxing from LA at midnight, since her two right hands got into the office in London at eight A.M. It turned out that this was very productive, since things were being accomplished literally around the clock.

Besides mold-makers and foam technicians, the team included pattern-cutters and painters, as well as many outside workers and companies, including one that made the little name tags for the suits, etched in metal. Don West's leather outfit had to be made by a fashion leather man. Burnham's team made the prototype, but they weren't satisfied with the results; Chay International stepped into the breach and took the costume a step further, much to Burnham's delight.

When she turned to the suits the cast would wear while exploring the *Proteus*, Burnham's quest for authenticity took her to the Ministry of Defense, which actually manufactured them. "My coordinator [Jeeda Barfoot] managed to persuade them they desperately wanted to do this," Burnham remembered, "and they did, they loved it."

The prototype for those suits, which were completely fabric and more straightforward than the cryo suits, were based on the Air Force g-suit. Stephen Hopkins wanted it to be very dark, so they made it black. But he also wanted it to catch the lighting in the wide shots. Burnham had a reflective finish put in behind a sort of mesh, so they would sparkle in the light.

"We made a couple of prototypes, and they looked good, but they didn't look like something that would *really* be worn on a space mission. It looked like a fashion thing." So it was off to the Ministry of Defense, with Burnham's design and the MOD's look. "We wanted it to look like it had been pushed through a big industrial machine, patterns that had been made on computer. They needed to look like standard objects, with a certain crudeness, but in the right way. Our things looked a bit self-conscious. It was quite funny, because the MOD designer, Giles, kept saying, 'I don't think we can do it as good as that,' and we were saying, 'But we *don't want* delicate work.' It took them a while to understand what we were actually getting at." Burnham was totally pleased

The *Proteus* exploration suits had to be made only for those actors who would be on the *Proteus* sets, except for Major West, who had his own helmet and "antique" leather gear.

with the result, and added massive boots of a kind that had actually been meant for Arctic expeditions.

The last area of costuming that Burnham had to think about was what the actors would wear on the planet the *Jupiter 2* crash-lands on. "Stephen didn't want to go too spacey," Burnham remembers. "He wanted a bit more street cred. The clothes they wear on the planet could be pretty contemporary—they didn't have to keep them alive or be insulated."

Burnham started with a spacesuit which she pared down in stages, continually refining it and then turning to a company in America called Spywork, which made police and airline uniforms as well as wet weather gear. "The set was very brightly colored," she says, "and it was important that those costumes be very neutral, so you could see them—otherwise they'd be like camouflage, and you wouldn't be able to see them against the set!" Burnham went for a plain color, sort of a gunmetal-bronze, and meant to suggest space-issue but more human—uniforms, but with options.

"The idea was, Penny would be wearing something that a teenager would feel cool in, but if her mother was wearing the same

thing, she wouldn't be like mutton dressed as lamb—she'd look elegant. So they had different versions. We found what people felt happy in. Lacey felt happy in her dungarees, Mimi liked her vest and pants, William had a slightly more formal, slightly militaryish look. And of course, Don West, he wore what he wanted to wear, which was the leather stuff. It was antique, his own individual stamp—something that could have been his grandfather's, customized for what he needed. If you look at the bubble-fighter suit, it's not space-age fabric like the planet stuff is, because the fabric for the planet suit is what they use for the fire department in the United States. It's fire-proof, waterproof, acid-proof, *everything*-proof. It's conceivable that on a space mission, Spywork might actually do clothing like that, clothing to move around in and look good in."

Aesthetics combined with practicality is how Burnham would articulate her primary tasks as a special effects costumer. Like Fellini, she says that the screen is made up of millions of details and that's what makes the picture. "To get something that people will look at and gasp—a car, a house, an item of clothing, pottery—it has to have quality to it," Burnham says. "Quality of thought, the creative bit—I don't know where that comes from. Inspiration, imagination, are so important. But when it's carried through as well as it possibly can be, you'll get something that's worthwhile."

For Burnham, one of the best parts of her job is working with other creative people as part of a team. "There are fine artists who are geniuses who can do things on their own," she says. "I'm not one of those. I wouldn't enjoy it. I think one of the wonderful things is working people. Because the creative process isn't all about the final product, it's the process that goes into it. We had a lot of fun. When you're communicating in ways with other people who have their own ideas—it's like water, it's all just moving. It just happens."

The *J2* exploration team on the *Proteus*. Vin Burnham persuaded the Ministry of Defense to manufacture the costumes, in order to convey the effect of a durable, industrial-strength look and texture.

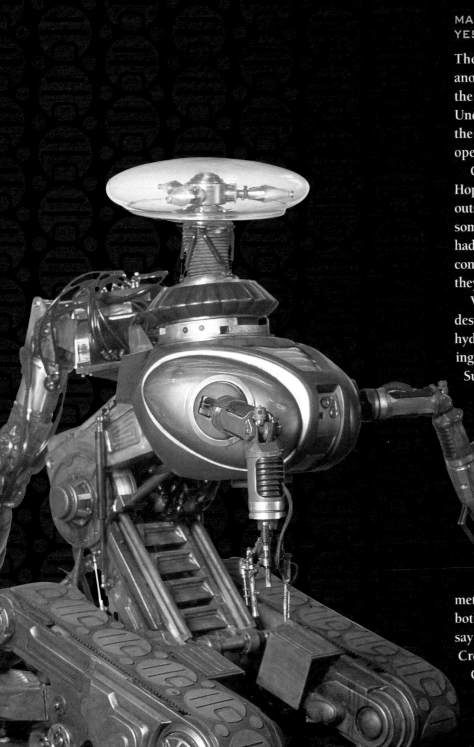

MAKE THAT ROBOTS.
YES, PLURAL.

The Jim Henson Creature Shop was another logical choice for the creation of the two robots featured in *Lost in Space*. Under the supervision of Verner Gresty, the shop not only built the robots, but operated them as well.

Gresty and his team met with Stephen Hopkins and Norman Garwood from the outset, to refine the robot designs into something practical. Hopkins and Garwood had strong visual ideas and were able to convey to the Creature Shop exactly what they wanted.

Verner Gresty would seem to have been destined to build robots. He started out in hydraulics and engineering design, studying physics at Guildford University in Surrey, later changing to electrical engineering when he found things getting too theoretical for him. He did some hydraulic engineering and then, through a friend, got into the film business by accident. His first movie was *The Hunger*, for Dick Smith, where his task was to help fill molds. For a while he worked freelance in the area of animatronics. Then Charles Stephenson, whom Gresty had met on the set of *Greystoke*, where they both worked with Rick Baker, phoned to say he had a new job as head of the Henson Creature Shop in London and would Gresty like to join him. Gresty did and never looked back.

Gresty's original idea for the robots involved a human in a suit, for the sake of direct access and communication. But when he and his team saw the designs and the scale, they knew there was no way they

The Robot as rebuilt by Will with the very familiar dome reminiscent of the original TV series.

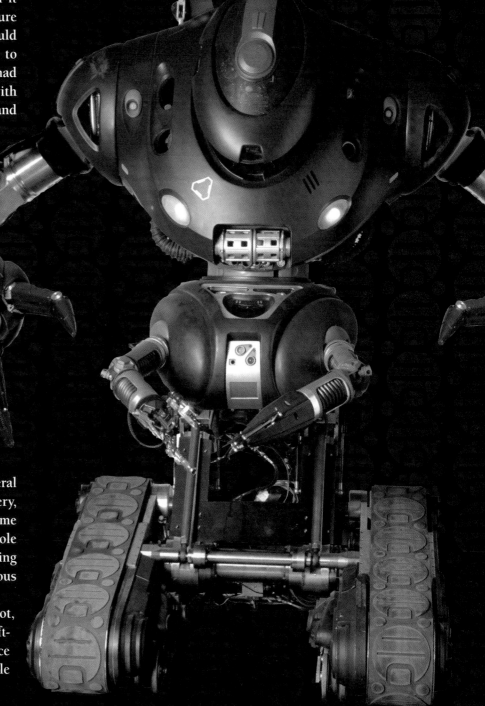

The full-size Robot produced by the Jim Henson Creature Shop awaiting action.

could get a person into it—it would have to be a mechanical device. But exactly how complicated a device could it be?

As all the designs came from Norman Garwood, Gresty and his team talked it over with him. They had to make sure that everything Garwood proposed could actually be made. Then they had to decide how complex to make it. "We had to decide whether it was a big thing with blobs coming off it," Gresty says, "and whether we'd have to physically push it up and down the set."

Early on, Gresty decided that because of time and economies, the second robot body would be mostly contained in the first one. "Robot Two is effectively the lower half of Robot One, but the tracks are slightly closer together," he explains. "It fits the script as well, since Will assembles the second robot from the spare parts left over from the packing bay. That makes it all logical. It would have to be the same sort of parts, so we decided we might as well make several sets." Installing lots of CAD machinery, hardware, and software, Gresty put some engineers on the case and had the whole thing designed in the computer, printing out actual-size schematics on enormous sheets of paper.

To control the operation of the Robot, Gresty took motion-control base software and added specific performance elements to it, giving the team a stable

The first of the two robots, about to meet its doom on the *Proteus*. Fans of the old television series were unsure how to react when first presented with the image of this eight-foot industrial machine.

computer platform for control. Four people working in tandem would operate the Robot. "One person would operate the tracks, by wire-link coming off it," Gresty explains. "There was something like a tank control, with joysticks, so it could be made to go back and forth at different speeds. Another person had to do the little arms, and that would be off a direct, a slave control tied to that person. It would be an exoskeleton which the performer would move around. Another person controlled the big arms, the waist movement, the way the Robot rocked back and forth

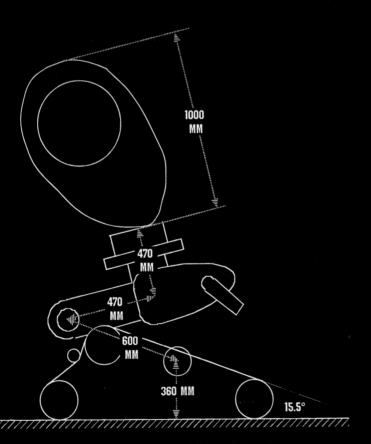

1000 MM

470 MM

470 MM

600 MM

360 MM

15.5°

Major West and the first robot, exploring the *Proteus*.

Scale drawing of Robot features for the workers at the Henson Creature Shop.

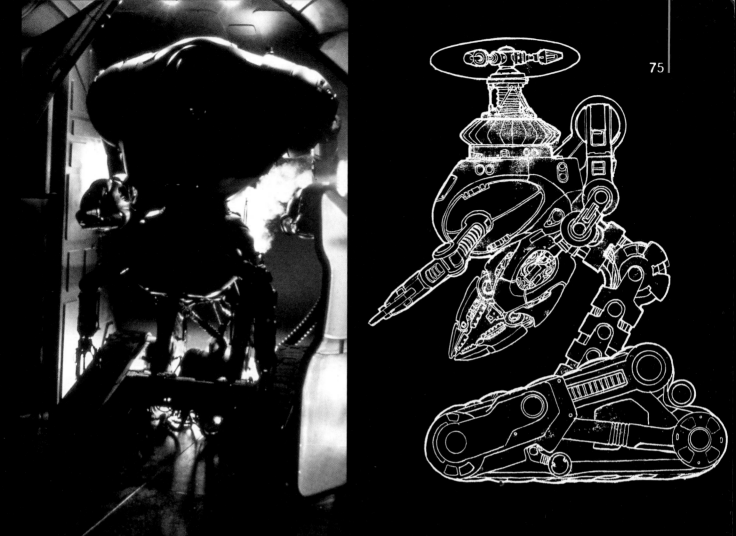

Side view (above) drawing of the second robot. Note similar treated structure.

Highlighted view (upper left) of the Robot emerging.

Dr. Smith (left) under attack by the "Steely Centurion" he has programmed to destroy the *Jupiter 2*.

More dramatic views (above) of the Robot's first appearance.

Details (inset, opposite page) of the size and reach of the Robot arms.

The Robot (opposite page) was a complicated mechanism built and maintained on set by the Henson Creature Shop. It weighed over a ton, which meant reinforcing the floor of the bridge in spots.

and the way it moved up and down on its scissors legs. A fourth person controlled the head, which could come out, look around, flash its lights, and so forth." With so many degrees of freedom, the areas of movement had to be partitioned off and assigned to different people—it was just too much for one person to control.

But how do four people go about making up one robot character? Very, very carefully, especially when it happens to weigh over a ton. Very carefully, and choreographically, according to William Todd Jones, the head robot performer. Though he has no objection to the term "puppeteer," "robot performer" is the term he prefers in this particular case.

Hopkins told Gresty that he wanted the Robot to be as free-ranging as possible so the actors could run around it and interact with it. Technical considerations dictated that there would always be a couple of lines coming out to the hydraulic power supply, and some sort of linkages for electronic signals, but all that could be either dressed away from the camera or lost in postproduction. Apart from that, the Robot became a free-ranging member of the crew, and, to Gresty's satisfaction, the actors began to relate to it as another character.

Creating that character was a task more delicate than one might think for Jones and the other robot performers. "You can anthropomorphize," Jones says, "but you have to be careful what you do. You have to set in some sort of character that people will recognize, of course, and have an emotional response to. There are little mannerisms, cocks of the head, so it has an emotional quality. It may look quizzical, or it may do something that people will recognize as indicating content, or being jolly, all sorts of things."

The first Robot, the larger of the two, was enormously difficult to maneuver, and it handled, Jones says, like a World War

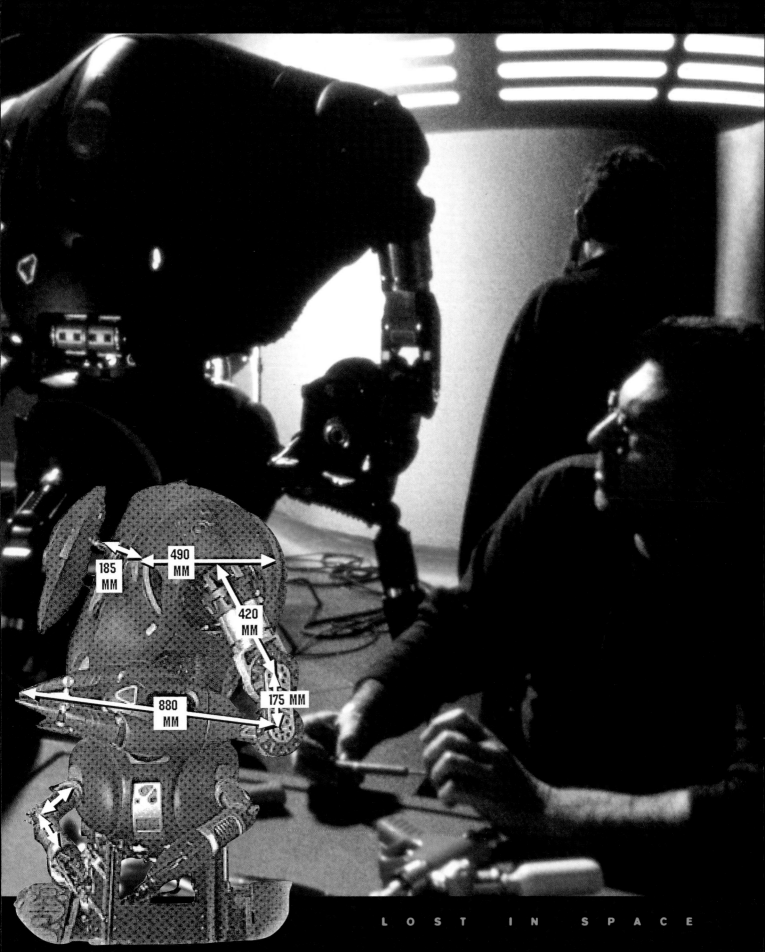

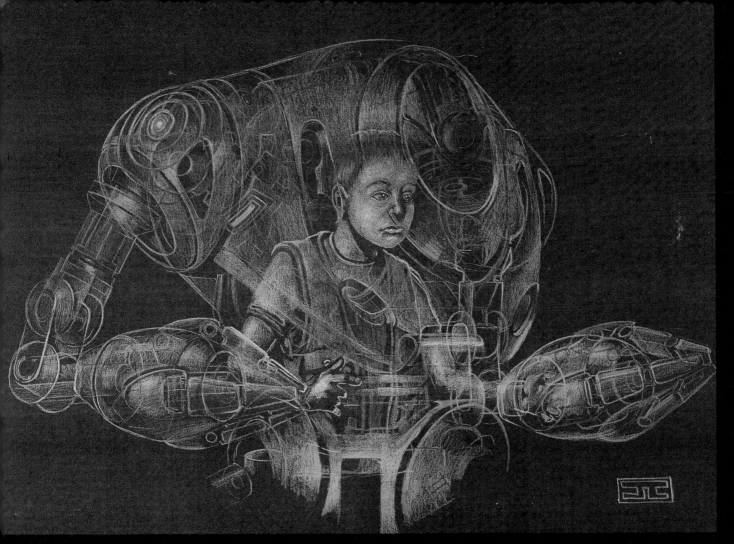

tank. On film, it seemed to be centered and solid and able to move about freely. In reality, getting it around the set was very difficult. The floors of the *Jupiter 2* bridge had to be reinforced before it could be allowed onto the set—there wasn't enough scaffolding in the areas where the hydraulic chairs were located, so the floors had to be reinforced bit by painstaking bit as the action moved farther along the set.

Jones describes the window of performance on a creature like this as being very small, the limits set by all the other elements involved. The performer controlling the caterpillar tracks had to be precise and hit his marks exactly, not just for the camera, but for safety's sake—no one wanted to run over Matt LeBlanc after carrying him in and dropping him on the floor, a move that all the performers, human and otherwise, spent hours perfecting.

It was a move that required Jones to straighten and bend one arm while in the remote-control rig, which, for reasons of space, camera angle, and noise, could not actually be on the set where the action was taking place. Jones and the three other robot performers were in a small space under the stage, watching the scene on monitors and listening through earphones. The other performers were also wearing their control rigs, for the sake of giving the Robot more animation and making it seem more, well, lifelike—so to speak.

Jones discusses the special challenges of having to act via remote control, when technical considerations require that the robot performers not be present on the set. "There isn't any direct feedback," he says. "With this, it's all sorts of different elements coming together, information coming in from various sources. I have two monitors—a wild camera that provides the view of the Robot I'd like to have if I could get close to it, and the main camera monitor, which is the shot to which I'm playing. Meanwhile, Verner is telling me when all the elements are coming together, when it's safe to move, because our view is limited to what the wild camera is seeing. We assemble all that information and hope that our timing is right."

The shot of the Robot dropping Don West on the floor, for example, lasts about three seconds in the film but took three hours to set up, plus rehearsal time. Matt LeBlanc's size and weight lying over a hydraulic arm wasn't the problem as such—it was the fact that the arm was capable of lifting four tons, and consequently, the performers had to be careful. "It's like being in a world where you've lost several of your senses," says Jones, "and you're trying to piece it together from what remains, to try to make some

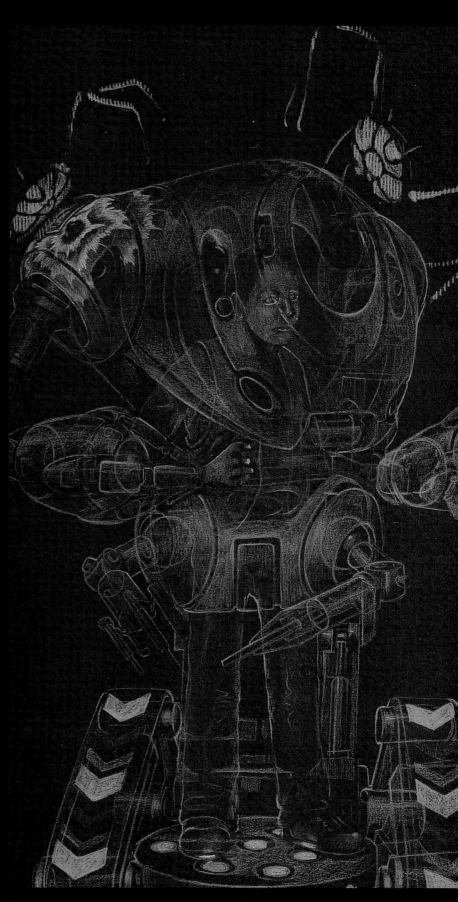

complete thing, something that worked."

Something that worked like an insect, at that; the first robot reminded Jones of a cockroach, while the second made him think of a praying mantis or a scorpion. The robots having elements of those things helped Jones and the other robot performers find and build characters for the robots, which is the sort of thing that will make an audience care about them as well.

He admits that the second robot really does have more of a character. As well, every fan of the original series will recognize the head, and Jones describes many of its movements as being more reminiscent of a human being. It's a direct contrast to the more powerful first robot, a mechanism that has more quirks, eccentricities, and weaknesses. "It was put together by an eleven-year-old boy," Jones notes, "and it looks like that and works like that."

To get into character, all the robot performers went through the script repeatedly as well as talking with Jack Johnson about what he thought the Robot should be doing and how it should work. The robot performers considered their relationship with all the actors to be important, since they made up two more characters on the *Jupiter 2*. The great amount of time needed to shoot sequences that would last only a few seconds onscreen meant that it was too possible for the performers to get separated from what the finished product was going to be—losing the forest for a fraction of one tree, as it were.

"Trying to keep that in mind was a constant process," Jones says. "It all had to be tied in to where the scene belonged in the whole of the movie, where the ups and downs were in terms of the performance, when he was good, bad, happy, all that. When did the Robot make a mess of things, when was he successful, when was

That bubble dome looks familiar . . .

The biggest challenge for the performers in manipulating the robots was having to perform motions without any sort of physical feedback in response to those movements. Needless to say, this was why watching every little move on the monitors was so important—nobody wanted to run over Matt LeBlanc.

sense of your world, so you can do any activity you want."

The lack of physical feedback made everything more difficult; Jones had to rely on muscle memory. "Potentially, the system could record the movement, so we could rehearse a few times, record each one, keep the movement recording that we wanted, and then we could play it back in the take. However, when we're working that close to an actor who may do something different, or something may go awry, the timing element is crucial. You are given that performance and you can't just play it back over and over again. You have to respond to what's happening there and then."

The characters of the robots were built up from how the cast related to them, but also from how the robot performers related to them as well. Jones confesses to playing favorites between the two, actually having a preference for the first robot. It was a feeling that he developed early on in the production and never lost. "It was like a well-loved motorcycle," he remembers. "You could press a button and it would do whatever you wanted, in a formidable way. It wasn't just the sheer power of it, though—there was a sense of it being a

It took a team of four performers to manipulate each robot. For the first robot, there was one person handling the treads, one handling the smaller arms, one for the larger arms and the waist movements, which involved not only rocking back and forth, but rising up and down on scissors legs, and one person to control the head.

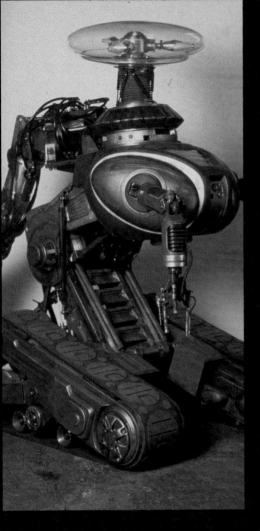

the other performers keep the real sequence in mind. "Stephen Hopkins also had to keep the line in his head, as did the rest of the cast," Jones noted. "Mostly, we all achieve it, and the normal line of events is visible."

Although there are technically only two robots in the movie, Jones and his team think of them as actually being four distinct ones. "There's the faceless machine that John Robinson has designed to be on board the *Jupiter 2* to sort out their problems," Jones says, ticking them off. "Then there's the reprogrammed one that Will has some control over, which fights spiders and saves the day—every kid is going to want that Robot! Then there's the second Robot Will builds from spare parts, and then the same Robot twenty years on, which has grown under the malignant gaze of Dr. Smith, any emotions long buried. Having seen the women killed, it could be in dramatic shock. But this ancient neural character is drawn out from its dim and distant past by a little boy who it's either going to kill or save. It has its moment and its internal struggle, and comes out as a sort of lovable, quirky, rusty, arm-in-a-funny-place scorpion-cum-human."

more of Jack's character involved in it . . ." The transitions the Robot went through were hard to keep in mind when shooting out of sequence.

Jones credits the first assistant director, Chris Carreras, with helping him and

Drawing of Robot and Will (top inset) showing the relative scale.

Will's new best friend.

The Robot Will constructs (top) from the spare parts in the robot bay, to house the "mind" of the first robot, downloaded during its destruction on the *Proteus*. Hopkins wanted it to resemble the Robot from the original TV series, as a tribute.

Will and the second robot: "Mom always said I should make new friends."

Sketch of the parts from which the Robot will be re-built.

Stephen Hopkins listens (oposite page) to Dr. Smith's opinion of the Robot, which hasn't improved over the decades.

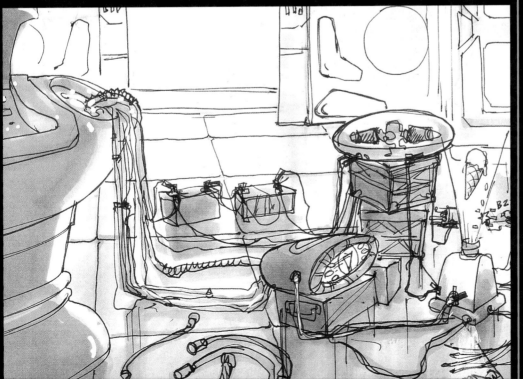

Norman Garwood: (opposite page, top) "We had to get everything to look believable, the finishes to look right, everything to look crisp and shiny."

A series taken during a crisis on the *Jupiter* bridge.

With the production of *Lost in Space* scheduled for nineteen weeks of filming at Shepperton Studios just outside of London, cast and crew settled in on eight soundstages, including two built so recently that the dividing wall had not yet gone up between them. Norman Garwood persuaded Shepperton management to leave the wall unbuilt to provide a larger-than-usual set for the alien planet the *Jupiter 2* would crash-land on.

By the time actual shooting began in March 1997, set construction had been under way for almost four months, following three months of sketching and brainstorming. The time of pure conceptualizing had come to an end—now it was time for realization and, where necessary, adaptation.

Construction of the *Jupiter 2* set involved every department. The ambition, as Norman Garwood described it, was to build the most up-to-date, prestigious spacecraft ever. "We had to get everything

to look believable, the finishes to look right, everything to look crisp and shiny," Garwood says, "and we had to do it in a certain amount of time. I felt that was the biggest problem—trying to get everything together by a particular date!"

Garwood describes that set as being the most problematical, for several reasons. Everyone was involved in its construction, which meant the area was crowded with builders and specialists. Complicating construction, however, was the fact that everything being built was, for all intents and purposes, a prototype. "It wasn't like a Georgian living room, where you know what it looks like," Garwood explains. "We were all trying things for the first time. No

one had ever done a cryotube before. Everything had to be tested, there was all this testing of colors. The set was mostly monochromatic, but with wonderful strong bursts of light and color rather than one big color thing. Also, the film would be on the bridge set for a fairly long time, so we had to maintain interest, we had to be careful not to give away too much of what was there or the audience would be thinking, 'Oh, we're still in here, are we?' You have to keep the mystery, keep the eye interested."

A good working relationship with the cinematographer is vital for making sure a set looks good, and lighting is positively crucial. "No matter what kind of set you do," Garwood says, "the cameraman can make it or break it. He can light it and it can look stunning, or he can light it and make it look like a supermarket. For me, I work very closely with the cameraman

because you know how you want it to look. You spend huge amounts of time with the cameraman, just thinking about what to do. Then you get something on the stage, you know what it's going to look like and it's a wonderful coming together of two minds. You've got to get together and have a plan and a vision." The *Jupiter 2* bridge lighting was actually built into the set itself, for the most part, which presented its own lighting techniques, challenges, and problems to solve.

Garwood's other big concern was the planet. "We didn't want it to look silly," he says. "We tried to have an element that would look believable, but not something that would have people thinking, 'Oh, they've gone down to whatever canyon to do that.' We didn't want it to look as if the Robinsons had gone off to a sand pit."

The process of visualizing the planet was, for Garwood, a very serious task. Often described as fanciful, he wanted to combine the elements of an alien world with just the right amount of crediblity. In the end, he found himself looking at microscopic photographs of hair follicles. "When I saw those," he remembers, "I thought, 'Planet! I like it!' Because these are real things, you can believe in them.

R efining the look (above) of the *Proteus* corridor.

A long corridor, made to look even longer by skillful use of lines and lighting.

The J2 exploration team look for signs of life on the *Proteus*. They're about to find it.

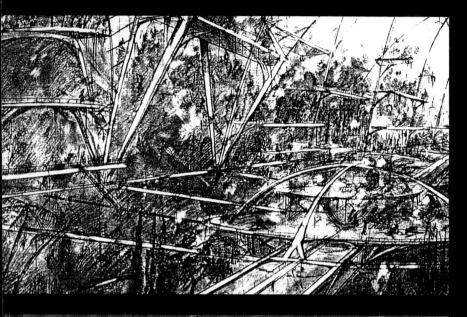

You change the sky, put a couple of little characters in there, you're in a huge forest. If you look at things like stuff on the planet, the trees and the pods, you accept them, you believe them because you've seen it somewhere in the dark depths of memory—that's a hair follicle blown up fifty million times."

What Norman Garwood saw as a forest had to be constructed somehow. The fabrication of the trees and pods, along with the rest of the sets, was the responsibility of Anna Pinnock, for whom *Lost in Space* was the first big movie project undertaken as the set director from beginning to end. Like Verner Gresty and others involved in this production, Pinnock went into the film business more or less by chance. She was still at university in America studying English and drama when she went to work on the Merchant-Ivory production of *The Bostonians*.

The only way to do a job like this," she notes, "is from experience. You have to go in as an assistant and learn it." She'd worked with Norman Garwood before on three other films, as well as on movies as varied as *Four Weddings and a Funeral* and *The Fifth Element*. She feels her experience on *The Fifth Element*, where she assumed the job of set decorator halfway through production, helped her a great deal in meeting the challenges of fabricating futuristic and/or alien sets.

The set decorator must deal with everything you see within a constructed set, which includes model-making as well

Detail of the hydroponics garden (top) on the *Proteus*.

Detail drawing of the exterior (middle) of the *Proteus*.

Design drawing (left) for the planet where the *Jupiter 2* crashlands.

The Robot (above) discovers it's on the spiders' menu.

Don West (above, right) in full battle regalia.

The *Proteus* exploration team takes a break.

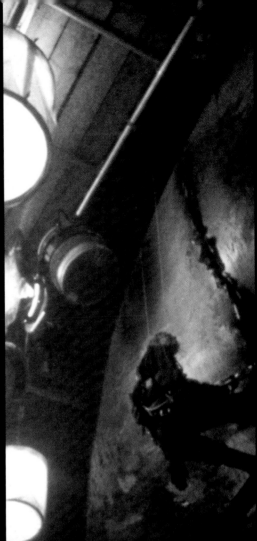

Q. What strange, exotic scene does Dr. Smith (upper left) see from his lonely prison cell aboard the now-crashed J2?

A. The film crew, of course, getting ready for another shot. Strange, exotic scenery to be added later.

An up angle shot of Judy Robinson (above) showing lighting and the part of the stage that will not appear on camera.

Stephen Hopkins (left) checks the horizon through a lens.

Judy: descent suspended, at least momentarily.

Penny Robinson, (far left) waiting to be filmed in her harness. Those big boots are the real thing—special effects costumer Vin Burnham found footgear made for Arctic expeditions.

Sketch of the re-built Robot. (inset)

Sketch of one area (right) on the planet.

Conceptual drawing of a time portal, (bottom) in various stages of opening and closing. The funnel shape is vaguely close to mathematical models of such things.

An early drawing (oppostie page, bottom) of the *Proteus'* design.

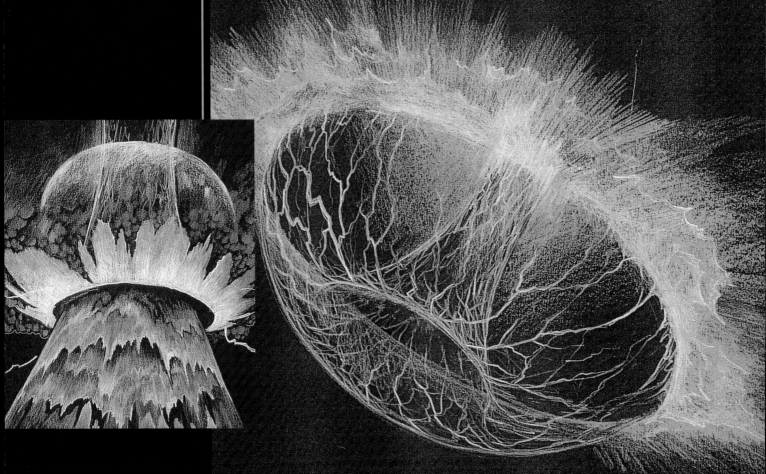

as literally decorating the full-sized finished product. She must also take charge of revamps—that is, when everything is taken out of the soundstage except for the basic structure of the set so it can be altered to look like a different area. The set for the alien planet was designed so large pieces could be pulled out and all the dressing removed. Then the colors would be changed completely and the set would be dressed all over again. "It was still the planet, but it was a different part of the planet," Pinnock explains. "It looked so completely different that no one will realize it's in the same physical space."

The dressing in the case of the planet set included the podlike plants, the swamp trees, the spaceship, the dressing on the spaceship, and the pipework and decay of the wrecked spaceship the Robinsons discover after inadvertently entering an area of time distortion—not to mention ground cover. "Construction really only gives you a painted set," Pinnock says, "which is the ground, the walls, and some pieces of sky."

Unlike the procedure on a period piece, where the entire set is handed over to the set decorator for finishing, it was necessary for Pinnock to work very closely with Garwood and Stephen Hopkins so she could follow their visualizations con-

Another time portal sketch. (below)

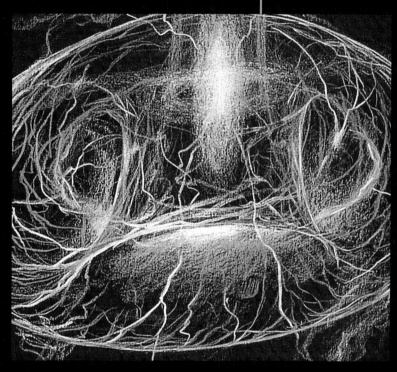

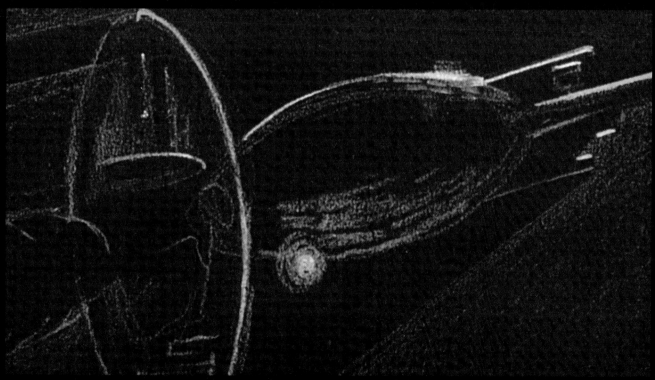

Every little move (right) that occurred between Matt LeBlanc and the Robot was choreographed to the inch.

Major Don West (below) finds out that what he thought was going to be a glorified baby-sitting job has become a matter of life, death, space, and time.

sistently. When it came to the matter of materials, she called on sculptors experienced with fantastic settings, who could work with latex, plaster, and fiberglass to deliver whatever texture might be required. The pod forest was fabricated chiefly by the modelers.

"The planet set was actually Pinnock's favorite kind of set dressing on this production. "All these ideas came from microsurgery," she explains, "where you have the most incredible shapes and images. It's a totally different tack than looking at rain forests. It's a much more interesting angle to come in at. I think that's been great, because we have just fabricated our own version of nature. The trees do look like trees, and we do use some real stuff, but not very much. Mainly we've made everything just by mucking around, dipping foliage in latex and seeing what we come out with. It's really been a whole process of experimentation and coming out with the right thing at the end of it. I've never done sets quite like that."

Dr. Smith (left) knows he can use Will's love for his father to manipulate the boy.

The explorers find that the future is literally closer than they thought.

Older Will is still very angry with his father for making them go on the J2 mission.

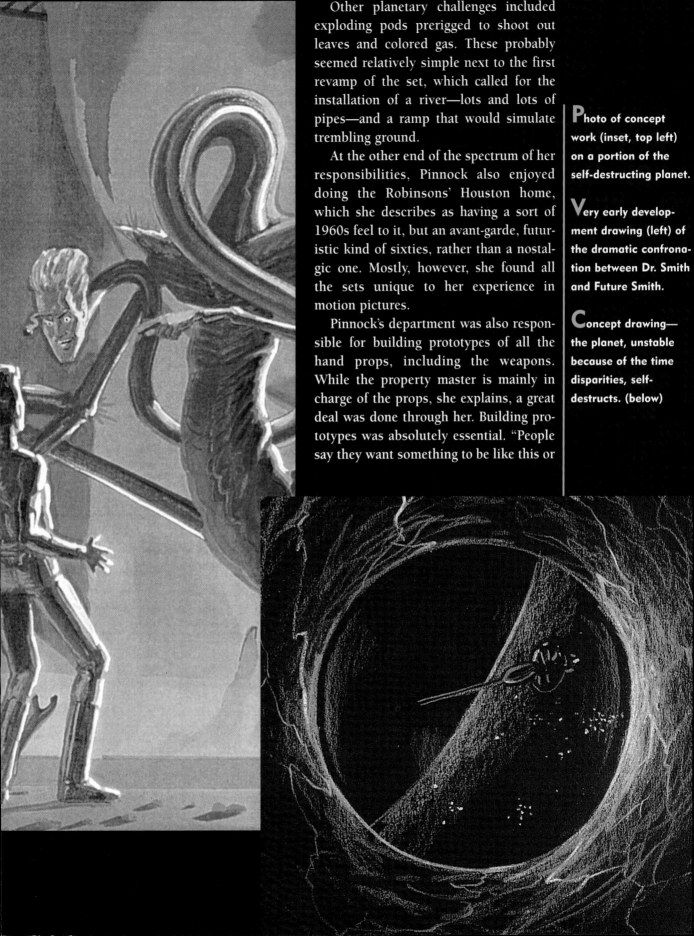

Other planetary challenges included exploding pods prerigged to shoot out leaves and colored gas. These probably seemed relatively simple next to the first revamp of the set, which called for the installation of a river—lots and lots of pipes—and a ramp that would simulate trembling ground.

At the other end of the spectrum of her responsibilities, Pinnock also enjoyed doing the Robinsons' Houston home, which she describes as having a sort of 1960s feel to it, but an avant-garde, futuristic kind of sixties, rather than a nostalgic one. Mostly, however, she found all the sets unique to her experience in motion pictures.

Pinnock's department was also responsible for building prototypes of all the hand props, including the weapons. While the property master is mainly in charge of the props, she explains, a great deal was done through her. Building prototypes was absolutely essential. "People say they want something to be like this or

Photo of concept work (inset, top left) on a portion of the self-destructing planet.

Very early development drawing (left) of the dramatic confronation between Dr. Smith and Future Smith.

Concept drawing— the planet, unstable because of the time disparities, self-destructs. (below)

Will and Dr. Smith (right) negotiate terrain that has changed suddenly thanks to the presence of time portals. This was the largest set on the lot.

Norman Garwood: (inset) "Microscopic photography, hair follicles—when I saw those, I thought, 'Planet! I like it!' The trees and the pods—you believe them because you've seen it somewhere in the dark depths of memory. That's a hair follicle blown up fifty million times."

A surprise for John and Will Robinson (below) —the Will Robinson who grew up marooned on the planet with Dr. Smith.

that, but they don't really know until it's right in front of their noses that it's not what they want at all. You have to do an enormous amount of prototype building on a film like this because the ideas are coming out of someone's head rather than from a reference. Period films require you to replicate a time, but when you're going from someone's brief, the brief may not be quite right. It's not until you see it in front of you that you realize it needs modifying or adding to or that you have to start from scratch. We spent a fair amount of time on all that, in order to get everything really right in the early days."

If *Lost in Space* is unique to Anna Pinnock's movie experience, she herself is somewhat unique in turn. Aside from

Two views of the pilot of the Sedition fighter from the opening space battle sequence.

having come to set dressing from a non-design background, she's one of those rare individuals whose eyes are actually two different colors. While this may have absolutely nothing to do with set decoration or knowing whether a prototype will succeed, it does tend to reflect the fact that she sees things in a different way.

Preliminary drawing for the dramatic action finale as the *Jupiter 2* flies through the self-destructing planet.

Dr. Smith (above) is about to meet his worst enemy.

Concept drawing—John Robinson falls through the right time portal to be reunited with his family.

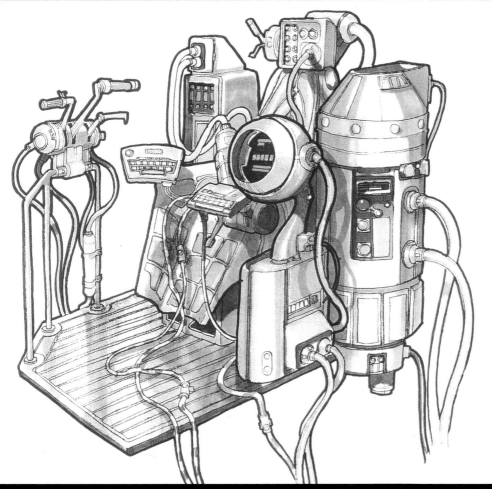

D rawing for older Will Robinson's time portal technology

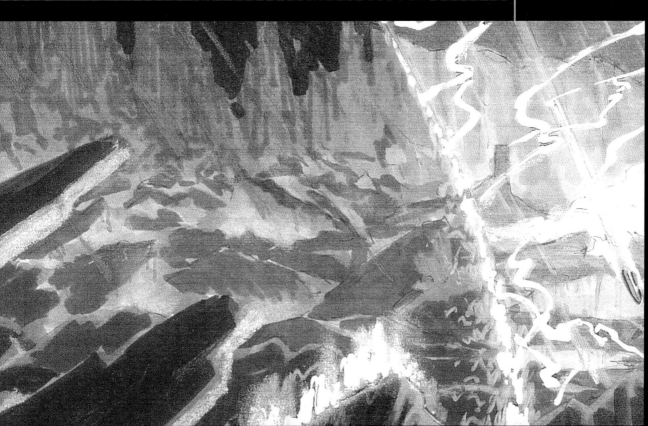

A full-form version made for brief long shots. Some of the puppeteers in their green/blue screen head-to-toe suits are visible, along with the rods, also covered in green material for removal in postproduction

Everyone who remembers the old TV series also remembers the Robinsons' pet, Debbie the Bloop. She seemed to belong mainly to Penny Robinson and bore a very strong resemblance to a chimpanzee with something fitted over her head to make her look like an alien animal—which, of course, was exactly what she was. Whenever Penny interacted with her, she made her own particular little sound: *Bloop!* Real nomenclature has, now and again, been based on similar kinds of things.

Anyone hoping to see a mutated chimpanzee filling the alien pet role in *Lost In Space* the movie will be disappointed. On the other hand, anyone hoping to see a rather unusual form of life is in for a treat, courtesy of the Henson Creature Shop.

Working from yet another set of Garwood designs, Verner Gresty and his team created designs of their own to render the Blawp in three dimensions. Or rather, Blawps—not just more than one for filming purposes, but two versions: one small, immature Blawp, and one gigantic eight-foot adult Blawp, who just happen to be the same Blawp, twenty years apart (those time ripples on the planet do tend to complicate matters).

Even Stephen Hopkins treated the Blawp as another actor on the set.

Gresty describes the small Blawp as being the next extension from a Muppet type of puppet, which is always a hand puppet; although the Blawp's body was manipulated by a team of puppeteers using rods, the head was literally packed with animatronics. The team discovered that they would have to make a version of the small Blawp that was actually twenty percent larger than the original, just for the sake of being able to pack even more animatronics into its head to get a greater range of expression in the face. "It's just for close-ups," Gresty explains, "because it has a lot more movement. For the real reactions and main expressions, you'll see a slightly larger Blawp, although you won't know it."

In other words, even the alien has a double.

The Blawp handling crew reherses on a stand-in.

Close-ups and details of a final-stage model for the Blawp.

Very early sketches (opposite page) for Blawp. Note that the name went through several stages of evolution.

Animatronics is a general word for mechanical animation. Most people associate it with Disneyland and Disney World, which uses animatronics in its most traditional form. In reality, however, the definition of animatronics can range from the *LIS* robots to the little Blawp. Little Blawp's expressions are the result of lots and lots of little servomotors moving a combination of silicon and foam latex.

It was actually similar in principle to how Todd Jones's robot performer teams manipulated the robots. The set of controls for the face was a big stick—a multi-access joystick operated through the computer system, so the puppeteer could dial up all the expressions and edit them in sections; for example, changing the eye movement without changing the mouth.

This editing more often than not took place on the monitor. "The face of little Blawp was Dave Barclay," Gresty notes. "We kept him next to the camera and the line of sight while the others operated the body. These shots were always fairly static, sitting on laps, eating a candy bar, so instead of mechanizing her, we just decided to remove the manipulation rods in postproduction. Mechanizing him was not really necessary for what we needed

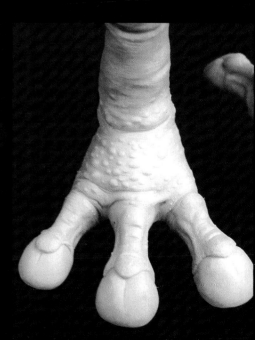

The little Blawp (immediate right) was actually more difficult to make than the big one; the machinery in the head was more complex.

The puppeteers (below) rehearsed long hours to learn to move together. The green rods, like the green screens, are invisible to the camera.

Twenty percent more Blawp to love: (opposite page) the Creature Shop built a slightly larger Blawp for close-ups. The larger head accommodated more animatronics, which allowed the face to be more expressive.

Blue Blawp, (inset) being readied for close-up work.

to do, in that any running and jumping shots had been planned as computer-generated shots from the outset."

As if that weren't complicated enough, the Creature Shop had to make five versions of her, in her various colors. "She's like a chameleon," Gresty explains, "she changes colors. She turns red when she's angry, becomes darker when she's scared, and so forth. Her neutral color is the yellow and blue version." In order to cover all the color schemes that appear in the film, Gresty had the shop make one head and then engineered backward from there.

Motors were inserted into the little Blawp's head by Richard Darwin, who was Gresty's head mechanic on the Blawp. Everything about that seemed to be a challenge. It wasn't just the fact that they had reached the limit of the number of motors they could load into a head that size, and thus had to build a larger one. The large oval eyes proved tricky as well—round eyes are much easier to engineer for blinking.

Meanwhile, the prototype had to be given to the puppeteering team as early as possible so they could rehearse with it and give Gresty feedback about the various problems and techniques of manipulation. Having rehearsal time just to learn how to move together as one creature was crucial; the robot performers' option of learning as they went just wasn't an option for the little Blawp's troupe.

Eventually, the puppeteers' movements began to mesh so well that it often seemed as if they were communicating telepathically. Even so, Gresty notes, it was impossible to get any shot with the little Blawp in just one take. "They had to go several times, there were so many elements to get right—individual arms, even fingers to be moved."

The most unusual sight, however, was the puppeteer troupe in their green suits, which made them, for all intents and pur-

It wasn't long before the cast began reacting to the Blawp as if it were a living creature.

Lacey Chabert's amazement at the big Blawp was genuine, as is Mimi Rogers's. Everyone enjoyed doing scenes with the big Blawp.

poses, invisible to the camera, just like a green screen. Most of the time the puppeteers were simply kept out of the frame, but with certain shots it was impossible to accomplish any action unless the puppeteers were around the little Blawp.

And as if all that weren't enough, the actors—the fully human actors, like Lacey Chabert, Jack Johnson, Heather Graham, and Matt LeBlanc—had to act with the little Blawp as if it was actually a skittishly intelligent, living creature that wasn't being maneuvered by several people with rods. For Lacey Chabert, the key was focusing on the intricacy of the face while allowing herself to slip back into the let's-pretend type of play she engaged in with her dolls when she was much younger.

Gresty praised the entire cast for the speed and ease with which they accepted the Blawps, along with the robots, as actual characters. Lacey Chabert's technique

Judy (opposite page) finally discovers what form the adult Blawp takes.

of focusing and allowing herself to believe the creature was alive was apparently not only exactly right, but contagious.

However, if she excelled in accepting the puppet as a live thing, Chabert outdid herself playing to a Blawp that wasn't even there—that is, a computer-generated Blawp.

"That was another element I'd never had to work with before," she recalls. "Having to act as if there was something crawling over me when it wasn't even there." Chabert would rehearse with little Blawp's other stand-in, a stuffed-animal type of thing called, appropriately enough, "Stuffy" by the cast and crew. "We rehearsed with it a lot," Chabert says, "but as soon as Stephen called action, they took it away and there was nothing there. So I would imagine it like my dog. I love my dog. I have a little miniature pinscher and he's a hypermaniac! He reminds me of the Blawp in some ways—all that energy. So when I had to do that, I would just imagine my dog. But it was difficult. I was always wondering if it was going to work, did it look real, was it like I was holding on to air? We watched a lot of playbacks. It was the sort of thing you just had to have fun with and use your imagination."

It might be easy to imagine, then, that the giant Blawp provided similar challenges in the giant economy size. But— surprise, surprise!—according to Gresty, the giant Blawp was much easier to make and is actually a simpler mechanism than the little Blawp. "All the giant Blawps we had to build were rod puppets on a giant frame. The arms were just big rods. It was far more mechanical and straightforward. Standing inside the giant Blawp was another performer, moving around and watching a TV monitor, with a separate puppeteer doing the face."

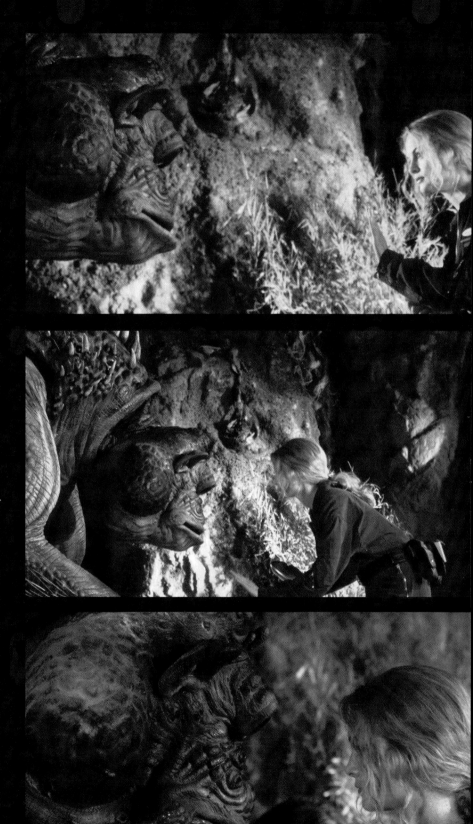

The *J2* seems to race through space. In fact, the camera is doing all the movement. Motion-control means being able to duplicate exactly those camera movements, as many times as necessary.

Every element in the sequence is a separate pass of the motion-controlled camera. The passes will be layered together to yield one incredibly detailed image.

For that matter, not all of it is actually life either—at least not in the outer space of *LIS*, as rendered by computer-generated imagery, all under the supervision of Angus Bickerton.

A visitor to the *LIS* set once mistook Bickerton for an intern, not because of any awkwardness, but because of his ten-dency to be right in the midst of any work to be done and his willingness to be as much of the team as he is the head of it. Then, too, there's his youthful appearance, which belies Bickerton's long list of cred-its, mostly in feature films. Bickerton has worked as a model unit camera operator, motion control cameraman, and live

action motion control cameraman; he was the visual effects coordinator for the *Space Precinct* TV series while working as visual effects director/supervisor on such films as *Time Runner*, *Crackerjack*, and *Cyberjack*. Just prior to going to work on *LIS*, Bickerton demonstrated his talent for visual effects design in *The Adventures of* *Pinocchio*, a movie that attracted a great deal of favorable attention, in good part because of those effects.

LIS reunited Bickerton with another Pinocchio alumnus, Magic Camera Company, whose offices are out at Shepperton. Magic Camera is only one of several studios that worked on computer-

Details of texture for the gantry towers.

Close-up drawing of the Houston launch dome showing mission control on the side.

Houston launch platform (immediate left) with the *Jupiter 1*.

Stephen Hopkins (lower left) talked with NASA about this particular launch.

Down angle (below) on the *Jupiter* in the launch dome—doors open.

Every fan (bottom) of the original series is going to recognize that spacecraft.

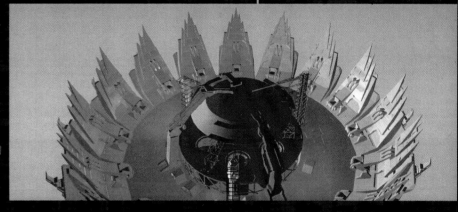

Close-up drawing (near right) of hyperdrive effect.

Drawing of (far right) hypergate ring.

Jupiter 2 (inset) approaching the apparently deserted Proteus.

The Jupiter launch (opposite page, bottom) tower at the moment the ship is taking off.

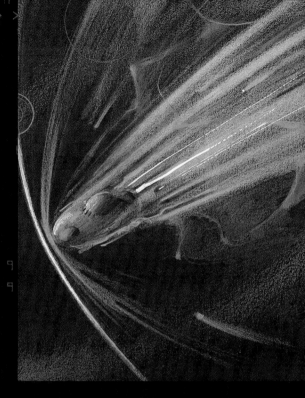

generated effects for *LIS*. Aside from the Henson Creature Shop, which handled technical tasks like rod-removal as well as integrating the animatronic Blawp with the purely computer-generated image that climbs all over Penny, another London company, VTR in Soho, produced a swarm of metal-eating spiders to menace the Robinsons on a miles-long derelict spacecraft called the *Proteus*.

The *Proteus* itself was created by the Magic Model Company, also based in Shepperton.

The man who crashed the *Jupiter 2* on the alien planet describes Ray Harryhausen as a personal deity.

Model unit effects director Steven Begg has been making movies for over fifteen years. One of his previous jobs was on *Aliens*, where he handled a small second model unit filming the atmosphere processor. Since then he has worked on numerous TV movies, cable TV movies, *Goldeneye*, the first Tim Burton *Batman*, and *Baron Munchausen*. He describes the *LIS* shoot, however, as being one of the longest and most painstaking, and the biggest, he's ever worked on. The crash of the *Jupiter 2* alone took about two weeks, requiring multiple cameras in various positions, and a staff of fifty to bring it off.

"We basically dragged and threw a twelve-foot model of the *Jupiter 2* into a miniature landscape in the backlot of Shepperton studios," Begg recalls. "The model had to simulate a craft that was supposed to be about three hundred feet long. To give it the mass and momentum of an object that big crashing across a landscape, I had to shoot at a hundred to a hundred twenty frames per second, and sometimes higher, depending on the action." That was, of course, after spending a few days standing around waiting for the famous British weather to clear.

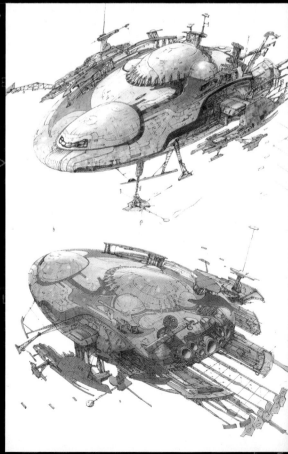

NOT ALL LIFE IN OUTER SPACE IS CUTE

Unless you've managed to avoid seeing any movies for the last two decades, you've probably seen motion control camera work in action. It involves the use of a computer-controlled camera making programmed moves, which, once saved as a computer file, can be repeated over and over again in precise duplication.

several times, perhaps as many as a dozen, depending on how many effects have to be added. Even the tiny lights on the *Jupiter 2* as it hurtles through hyperspace are an effect added during a separate pass of the motion-controlled camera—the *Jupiter 2* model itself has no lights built into it.

If that isn't complicated enough, there's

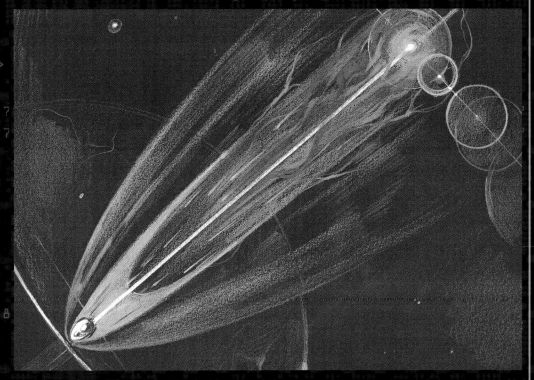

Jupiter 2 (far left) fleeing the explosion of the *Proteus*.

Jupiter 2 (far bottom) crashing on the planet.

Long range drawing of hyperdrive effect.

"Using a computer-controlled camera to do programmed moves past a model of the *Jupiter 2* will make it look as if it's flying to and from the camera," Angus Bickerton explains. "We use the fact that the camera can repeat those moves exactly so we can get separate passes to add lights, mattes, and other elements for compositing later on." Some of the other elements included computer-generated creatures such as little Blawp, courtesy of the Henson Creature Shop, and the infamous metal-munching, hull-burrowing spiders created by VTR, in Soho.

So, there's a bit of information you might not have known: the spacecraft isn't moving, it's the *camera*. And not just once, but

always the city of Houston—the model city, that is, of Houston in the *LIS* future. The set of Houston took up most of a soundstage at Shepperton, where Steven Begg's model unit team assembled the model in front of the camera. Everyone labored over details on the buildings and miniature highways, adjusting the lighting intensity and/or changing the angle while Begg, Nigel Stone, and Angus Bickerton constantly checked the progress through the camera lens.

Anyone who walked in cold to this set might have had trouble determining job titles, as everyone pitched in wherever help was needed. Angus Bickerton was just as likely as one of the gaffers or car-

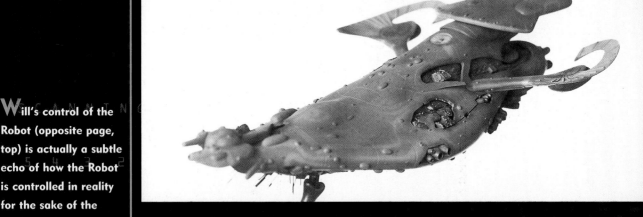

Will's control of the
Robot (opposite page,
top) is actually a subtle
echo of how the Robot
is controlled in reality
for the sake of the
movie.

Head robot performer
William Todd Jones:
"The robot performers
are living the fantasy,
while Will is playing out
that fantasy—squishing
space spiders with your
arms and feet." Will
Robinson: "Good-bye,
Robot."

penters to have been dripping watery black paint over a roadway that looked too clean for a planet supposedly choking on its own pollution. Art director Dave Warren dismantled and reassembled parts of the city as needed for camera position; it was all very much a group effort.

While shots were being set up, however, camera operator Mark Gardiner usually had to maintain his position not behind the camera, but behind a computer keyboard and monitor. Gardiner has nearly twenty years of experience in this sort of motion control, and has worked on twenty-two feature films. His task was to program the actual moves the camera would make for each motion control shot.

"Nigel sees what it needs to do, Angus programs the move, and I put all the coordinates in the computer," he explains. "All the data is kept in an ASCII file, and the file can then be used in digital houses to do the same kind of move. So when they composite it, they can put it all together and can match the move. The live stuff will be married with digitized electronic work. Angus knows what bits to shoot and how to shoot them and how to put it all together." As high-tech as all this may be, Gardiner says that inevitably a fair amount of motion control camera work depended almost as much on a bit of bungee as it did on precise coordinates. "Software and hardware has gone light-years ahead, but the mechanical side of it is—" He laughs.

"Well . . . the camera has to be weighted correctly, or you could lose the position."

Gardiner's first experience with motion control was back in the early 1980s, developing a ride called Space Journey for Joseph Strick and the TransLux Company. The audience/participants sat in plane simulators, much like the ones pilots train in. Motion control, Gardiner says, is really coming into its own now because all the information can be saved on a disk in a format compatible with all the electronic studios, like VTR and Magic Camera, who do so much work on feature film postproduction.

Model unit shooting, even without motion control, has its own set of problems and challenges. For one thing, it has to be very, very *slow:* one frame per second. "That's for the sake of depth of focus," Gardiner explains. "Live action filming runs twenty-four frames per second, but what you need to do on a model is keep everything in focus, like in real life. If we shot at live action speed in here, there wouldn't be enough light to do that. To use normal light, you have to stop the lens down because you need a smaller iris. If you focused on the roadways at regular speed, it would look like a model. That's because if you look at a real-size road, you wouldn't see parts of it out of focus. That's the trick in model work—everything has

to look real, real sharp, or it gives the game away." According to Gardiner, Nigel Stone had the hardest job, since the lighting for the model had to be scaled, which was time-consuming and difficult.

Setup for one shot could take two days, Begg says. "We set it up, shoot a test, and then the following day we get it right. The test would be for exposure, lighting, aesthetics, and action, if there is any." The take itself, with the camera shooting at a speed of one frame per second, would on average last about a minute and a half.

"At one frame per second, the camera is moving appropriately slowly," Begg continues. "But when that is projected at twenty-four frames per second, it will appear to be a real-time move. The computer compensates for the slowness of the camera in its calculations by slowing the actual physical movement of the camera down. It's like controlled Harryhausen, except that the camera is moving, not the model."

Motion control is not really all that new, Begg adds. A very simplified version was used in *2001: A Space Odyssey.* "But *Star Wars* and *Close Encounters of the Third Kind* really showed it off."

Such meticulous attention to detail does actually pay off. Footage of model future Houston seen lit up in a night shot is convincing, even in its raw, not-yet-composited state. Viewing this footage would be comparable to visiting a recording studio and listening to a song by playing the unmixed tracks one at a time.

The Robinsons' hometown is seen relatively briefly at the beginning of the movie, but it is pretty much the only sight audiences get of that future Earth. Houston has to stand in for the entire world; by looking at Houston, it's expected that audiences will unconsciously accept the premise of an Earth polluted and poisoned, of humanity heading for its last gasp. There's no way to produce that sort of response in moviegoers except by making sure even the smallest details are exactly right.

A spider emerging (left) from hiding. Note the double triangle structure.

Easily mistaken for a piece of detailing (inset below) of decoration, this is a spider in repose, before unfolding.

Detail drawing of spider eye (left) extruding from position of repose.

OR "OH, THE PAIN...THE PAIN!"

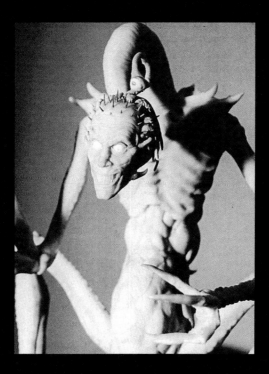

When Angus Bickerton first went through Akiva Goldsman's script for *LIS*, he managed to take it from six hundred visual effects down to 508. But only briefly: "This being a full-blown science fiction adventure," Bickerton notes, "it wasn't long before the number of visual effects passed seven hundred."

For some idea of just how high that number is, keep in mind that *Jurassic Park* ran to just over four hundred of those shots, T. rex included.

Much of that was due to the fact that there were so few plain shots in the film—almost every shot included at least a bit of green screen area. As Lacey Chabert recalled, "On the bridge, we'd just stare at the green screen while Stephen [Hopkins] yelled, 'An explosion!' and 'Spinning through the air!' and 'Crashing on the planet!' Stephen was great about giving us images to think about."

Seven-hundred-plus visual effects is no

small number of images to think about, let alone keep track of, as Stephen Hopkins and Angus Bickerton managed to do. The most dramatic of them, however, may well be the fate that befalls Dr. Zachary Smith. *Sort of* Dr. Smith, as played by Gary Oldman. Or, in the case of this particular sequence, it may actually be more accurate to say that *sort of* Dr. Smith will be played by *sort of* Gary Oldman.

"This is a new area of filmmaking, really," Bickerton remarked, "in that we are potentially doing a synthetic actor—a synthespian."

The fact that Dr. Smith's accidental, and unknown, spider scratch sustained on the *Proteus* causes him to mutate into a spider-human hybrid was in Akiva Goldsman's script from the beginning. Thanks to the time ripples on the alien planet, Dr. Smith gets to come face-to-face with his future self, Future Smith, who has spent the last twenty years marooned

These maquettes were sculpted as part of the conceptualizing process.

The design for Future Smith's face went through a great many versions before being finalized.

Angus Bickerton: "Stephen Hopkins came up with a very tall, thin, gaunt thing, like Nosferatu, the original 1920s vampire, but still half man, half spider."

with a bitter Will Robinson. Now in his thirties, Will is obsessed with perfecting his time machine so he can return to Houston and prevent the family, who are all dead, from going on the mission, thus saving their lives, and saving himself two decades with only Dr. Smith for company. (Oh, the pain, indeed.)

Except, of course, that just on the other side of a time ripple, the family are all alive and trying to get the *Jupiter 2* off the planet in a hurry, since the whole thing is literally tearing itself apart. Not that Dr. Smith cares about any of this—the only person making the trip back will be Dr. Smith, who finally reveals himself as the mutant Future Smith. "I am no mere man," Smith tells them. "I am a god!"

And a pregnant god (ahem) at that— Future Smith has an egg sac, almost ready to hatch out a multitude of metal-eating, practically invulnerable alien spiders who will conquer the Earth and eat the leftovers.

In a situation like this, a rubber suit from General Stores just isn't going to cut it.

"Stephen came up with a very tall, thin, gaunt thing," Bickerton remembers. "Like Nosferatu, the original 1920s vampire, but still half man, half spider—half the spider we had created early on in the film. The original intent was to create prosthetic makeup for Gary Oldman, to shoot Gary on the stage on a variety of different rigs that would give him the correct movement if he were half man, half spider. We'd film him against a green screen, take his head and attach it to a computer-generated Future Smith body."

After going through all sorts of changes on the Future Smith makeup, however, neither Gary Oldman nor Stephen Hopkins was happy with the way it turned

out. "So at the eleventh hour and fifty-ninth minute," Bickerton says, still wincing about it, "we changed our plan to something much braver, something that hasn't really been done before. There are things *like* this happening, but nothing to this extent.

"Ostensibly, we are going to motion-capture a facial performance from Gary for a computer-generated Future Smith." No wincing now; it was easy to see that the challenge appealed to him. "We've taken the maquette of the new Future Smith head design and we've had that cyberscanned, which is a system where two lasers rotate around the device and they shine a light out onto the surface. By interpolating the offsets in a computer, we end up with a complete three-dimensional map of the face, a huge mesh shape of the Future Smith face.

For Gary Oldman, who had worn plenty of heavy, prosthetic makeup in previous films, the prospect of not having to sit for hours in a makeup chair had a lot of appeal. He was also fascinated by the whole idea of what Bickerton called "capturing Gary's essential performance."

On a cool afternoon in mid-autumn, after the lunch break, Gary Oldman and Stephen Hopkins arrive at a Shepperton Studios soundstage which lots and lots of computer equipment, plenty of monitors and cpu's, and plenty of people to tend to it all. In the center of the room, six cameras are set up around a chair, which is facing yet another monitor. No one is sitting in the chair yet, but standing just behind it is a young man holding something that looks like a swizzle stick with bumps on it, stirring the air over the seat as if he were really mixing up molecules, or trying to make tiny dust particles swirl around tornado-style.

What the man is really doing is calibrating the area where Gary Oldman will

Gary Oldman being cyberscanned for a three-dimensional computer map of his head. Puture Smith features to be added later.

Angus Bickerton: "Once we've got the three-dimensional Gary Oldman performance recorded in the computer, we can apply that to the cyberscanned Future Smith head."

Future Smith—a creature conceived as being both more and less than human.

Dr. Smith: "I never liked me anyway."

be sitting. The bumps on his stick are painted with the same highly reflective material that coats the five millimeter balls now being carefully glued onto Oldman's face. The cameras are running at about sixty hertz, which is sixty pictures a second, which enables photogrammetry, or triangulation. Three cameras look at the same point and work out the space. That data can then be captured and turned into cyberspace—space in the computer. At the moment, the man is calibrating the accuracy of the photogrammetry with the rod. By stirring the air, he fills the zone full of dots—that is, he imposes a matrix on the actual space.

Sheila Dunne, working with VTR and the Film Factory, is one of the people looking after the whole computer-generated character. As VTR is also doing the computer-generated spiders, she is familiar with what they're supposed to look like, with the quality of their movement, speed, and so forth. She has also studied a lot of footage of Gary Oldman very carefully, to familiarize herself with his posture, movements, gestures, expressions—everything that portrays him as the actor playing Dr.

Smith. Observant and alert, Sheila has noticed that he has a certain twitch of the head that is quite specific to him.

His face now covered with little balls, Gary Oldman sits down amid the six cameras. While Stephen Hopkins, Akiva Goldsman, and lots of computer image experts watch Oldman's images, Oldman is watching the monitor in front of him, which will be playing back scenes he has actually already shot, in a manner of speaking. Which is to say, he's done the lines with older Will Robinson and with John Robinson, and moved around the set in the general way an actor will when playing a dramatic action scene.

Now he has to do all the lines again, including his death howl, responding either to older Will or John Robinson, pretending that the images on the television are really there for him to react to and be part of. With dots on his face, no less. Gary Oldman's concentration is such that he manages to do it for several hours, the entire afternoon, giving Stephen Hopkins and the computer imagery people no fewer than three takes per sequence of lines, and sometimes more.

The human element is being applied in different ways here," Sheila Dunne says. "You look at human faces all the time, so that's one human element that is instantly recognizable. You have to retain the human emotion. Otherwise, you'll know something's wrong.

"Stephen Hopkins wants to capture expressions as well as motion—anger, surprise, things like that. You can animate them, but they won't look the same. What we're trying to capture here is a performance, not do animation. You can animate everything from the neck down, but you have to capture the face."

Future Smith is lunch. John has told Will he loves him. The *Jupiter 2* has escaped the disintegrating planet. Penny kisses Don. The Robot has a starmap to Alpha Prime. Everything would be perfect, except for the fact that the planet's gravity field has collapsed and is about to suck the *Jupiter 2* into the cosmic equivalent of a trash compactor. Their only chance to survive is to use that hyperdrive again. Of course, this means they're going to get lost . . . again.

Will they ever get home?

When asked, Lacey Chabert claims to have no idea, although she does point out, quite logically: "If they do, *LIS* will be over!" Speculating on the next five years of Penny's life lost in space, Chabert acknowledges that while Penny does soften a little in the course of the story, she doesn't actually realize that she has, and she remains outwardly spunky and mischievous. Inwardly, however, she has come to care less and less about her hair and her clothes and her *Vogue* magazines. Even so, Chabert doubts that Penny will ever really enjoy being on the *Jupiter 2*, and will probably go out of her way now and again to let the people around her know she doesn't like it. But being the kind of girl she is, she will find ways to make it interesting for herself, to try to make it as exciting an adventure as any episode of "Penny Robinson: Space Captive" can be.

As for Chabert herself—would she go into space?

"After filming *LIS*, no! Negative on that!" She grins. "Houston, we definitely have a problem."

Jack Johnson, on the other hand, thinks the Robinsons will eventually find their way back to Earth. "Probably when I'm in my teens," he speculates, as always, referring to himself and the character of Will Robinson interchangeably. As well he might—like Will, he's very interested in computers. Since civilization hasn't

caught up with the technology of *LIS* yet, he doesn't have a holographic projector to play with, but he does have his own website. And when the call came for him to read for the part, he was already building a robot.

Jack is fortunate enough to differ from Will in having a far better relationship with his father, however, though Jack does assert that the problems between the older and younger Robinsons are of the sort that wouldn't be limited by an era. "Those problems could come up any time," he says.

But he doubts that they'll come up much between Will Robinson and any son he might have in the future. "If Will has a boy or something, he'll pay a lot of attention to him," Jack says confidently, "because he won't want his boy to feel like he did."

Unlike Lacey Chabert, Jack Johnson would go into space, just to satisfy his curiosity as to what's out there: "I'd like to see it." He admitted also to wanting to feel weightlessness. Interestingly, Jack also said he'd prefer going into space with his family than with a team of astronauts. If his family were trained, he says, "that would be much better than just taking people off the street."

Besides Future Smith, Jack was the only other cast member to meet "himself" twenty years on. It was "kind of weird," he explains, but also "kind of neat." His favorite part of making the *LIS* movie, however, was getting to do some of his own stunts. He also felt that Akiva Goldsman had given him one of the best lines in the film, which he delivers while building the second robot after the destruction of the original. When the second robot is complete enough to ask Will why he is rebuilding him, Will replies, "Mom always said I should make new friends."